W9-AHE-484

# HUMPHREY
# BOGART
## The Man and His Films

# HUMPHREY BOGART:
## The Man and His Films

**By Paul Michael**

*The Bobbs-Merrill Company, Inc.*
*A Subsidiary of Howard W. Sams & Co., Inc.*
*Publishers*

*Indianapolis*
*Kansas City*
*New York*

By the same author

**The Academy Awards:**
**A Pictorial History**

*Grateful acknowledgment is made to the
following for supplying photographs and other
invaluable assistance in the preparation of this
volume: John Sutherland, Max Bercutt,
Warner Brothers; Frank Rodriguez, 20th
Century-Fox Film Corp.; Paul Kamey,
Universal Pictures Company, Inc.; Harold
Danziger, Columbia Pictures Corp.; Mike
Hutner, United Artists Corp.; Mike Berman,
Paramount Pictures Corporation; Mark Ricci,
The Memory Shop; Joe Longo, Museum of
Modern Art; Roy George; Warren J. Dawson;
Loraine Burdick; Eloise Coates; Karla
Davidson, Metro-Goldwyn-Mayer; Jean
Andreola; Minnie Barnett.*

## Nobody Dies Like Humphrey Bogart

Casual at the wheel, blinding rainstorm,
The usual blonde doll alongside—only
This time our man knows she's talked,
The double-c, and by his cold eyes
We can tell it's the end of the line for her.

It's all in the corner of his mouth:
Baby if we're gonna go we'll both go
My way, and his foot deep on the gas
With the needle (close-up) leaping to eighty.
She's shaky but ready to call his bluff.

Rain and the wipers clearing the glass
And dead ahead the good old roadblock.
Quick shot moll—the scream forming.
Quick shot Bogey—that endearing look
Which was his alone, face and soul.

*Any way we go, baby, one or the other,*
*You'll look a lot prettier than me*
*When we're laid out in the last scene,*
*You in pink or blue with the angels,*
*Me in the same scar I was born with.*

Norman Rosten

From the forthcoming *Thrive Upon The Rock*,
by Norman Rosten, to be published by Trident Press.

# CONTENTS

*Nobody Dies Like Humphrey Bogart* by Norman Rosten **5**

**The Man** **9**

**His Films** **29**

**Index** **181**

*A Devil With Women*    31
*Up The River*    32
*Body And Soul*    35
*Bad Sister*    36
*Women Of All Nations*    39
*A Holy Terror*    40
*Love Affair*    43
*Big City Blues*    44
*Three On A Match*    47
*Midnight*    48
*The Petrified Forest*    51
*Two Against The World*    52
*Bullets Or Ballots*    55
*China Clipper*    56
*Isle Of Fury*    59
*The Great O'Malley*    60
*Black Legion*    63
*San Quentin*    64
*Marked Woman*    67
*Kid Galahad*    68
*Dead End*    71
*Stand-In*    72
*Swing Your Lady*    75
*Men Are Such Fools*    76
*Crime School*    79

*The Amazing Dr. Clitterhouse*   80

*Racket Busters*   83

*Angels With Dirty Faces*   84

*King Of The Underworld*   87

*You Can't Get Away With Murder*   88

*Dark Victory*   91

*The Oklahoma Kid*   92

*The Return Of Dr. X*   95

*The Roaring Twenties*   96

*Invisible Stripes*   99

*Virginia City*   100

*It All Came True*   103

*Brother Orchid*   104

*They Drive By Night*   107

*High Sierra*   108

*The Wagons Roll At Night*   111

*The Maltese Falcon*   112

*All Through The Night*   115

*The Big Shot*   116

*Across The Pacific*   119

*Casablanca*   120

*Action In The North Atlantic*   123

*Thank Your Lucky Stars*   124

*Sahara*   127

*Passage To Marseille*   128

*Conflict*   131

*To Have And Have Not*   132

*The Big Sleep*   135

*The Two Mrs. Carrolls*   136

*Dead Reckoning*   139

*Dark Passage*   140

*The Treasure Of The Sierra Madre*   143

*Key Largo*   144

*Knock On Any Door*   147

*Tokyo Joe*   148

*Chain Lightning*   151

*In A Lonely Place*   152

*The Enforcer*   155

*Sirocco*   156

*The African Queen*   159

*Deadline—U.S.A.*   160

*Battle Circus*   163

*Beat The Devil*   164

*The Caine Mutiny*   167

*Sabrina*   168

*The Barefoot Contessa*   171

*We're No Angels*   172

*The Desperate Hours*   175

*The Left Hand Of God*   176

*The Harder They Fall*   179

# THE MAN

HUMPHREY BOGART died at two o'clock in the morning on January 14, 1957. He had finally succumbed to the tenacious cancer that had been eating at his body. And with his physical death, something else died—a human quality that had captured the minds and imaginations of the entire world.

"Bogart is a man with a past," wrote French critic André Bazin. "When he comes into a film it is already 'the morning after'; his face scarred by what he has seen, and his step heavy from all that he has learned, having ten times triumphed over death, he will surely survive for us one more time."

Bogart has survived.

No one who ever saw him will forget the elongated face with subtle interweavings of wrinkles; the forehead anxiously creased; the deepening hollows under the eyes; the nostrils contracted; folds leading in to the slightly protruding mouth; the narrow upper lip; the thin, bony body, its poses reduced to the essential—gnarled and sober gestures.

His wife, Lauren Bacall, or Betty as he called her, was with him at the end. His two children, Stephen and Leslie, were in the house also. Just twenty-four hours before, he had slipped into a peaceful coma. No pain, no suffering at the end—just death.

In the many months of his illness, Bogart didn't seem to believe that he would die. It was not that he dodged the idea, that he pushed it from his mind. It simply could not penetrate his brain that he would be forced to leave all the things that he loved so much, things he had so recently found: his wife, his children, his work, his boat. Rather, thoughts of what he would do when he recovered flooded his mind.

In February 1956, Bogart entered the hospital at the insistence of his doctor. He had just completed what was to be his last film, *The Harder They Fall*. There was an operation and then intensive radium treatments. On December 25, in time for his birthday, he was permitted to go home. But it was only a matter of time. He could no longer hold the phone or lift his glass. On January 3, a rumor swept Hollywood, and a premature newspaper story stated that he had fallen into a coma and was about to die. Bogart gathered up his strength and dictated an open letter to the American press:

"I have learned with certain pleasure that both my lungs have been removed and that I have only a half hour to live. I am fighting death in a hospital which never existed. Others have given assurances that my heart has been removed and that it has been replaced by an old gas pump.

"They have buried me in practically all the cemeteries which exist, from here to Mississippi, including those especially reserved for dogs.

"All of this has greatly disturbed my friends, not to mention the insurance companies. That is why, following the rules of American government to 'Tell the truth and let the people judge for themselves,' I have decided to give certain explanations:

"I have a slight tumor in the esophagus, and in order not to oblige you to look in the dictionary, I advise you that it is the tube which goes from the throat to the stomach.

"The operation was successful, that is to say, in the fight between it and me, it was the tumor that quit. All that I am lacking is about thirty-three pounds, and I am sure that a good number of you would be ready to grant them to me. I propose therefore that someone open a 'bank account' in pounds in my favor. And I will not be hard on the parts of your bodies from which they could come."

There was Bogart near the end with his sardonic humor intact.

The question remains, did he believe that the cancer in his throat was only a tumor? Did he really believe that the weight he had lost was a fit subject for humor?

Betty had known the truth from the very day of the operation, and yet she never revealed her secret. She knew that it was a matter of a year or two at the very best. She knew that her husband would never make another film.

The people around him near the end knew, even though they had never been told. They laughed with him—Sid Luft, Judy Garland, Frank Sinatra, John Huston, Valerie French, Betty—the members of the so-called Holmsby Hills Rat Pack. They tried to keep his spirits up. Betty had continued to work on *The Designing Woman* so that he would not become alarmed.

John Huston told of the last terrible days:

"He was stretched out on the couch. Later, at five o'clock, he shaved and put on a pair of gray flannel trousers and a red smoking jacket. Then, since he could no longer walk, his emaciated body was placed in a wheel chair and pushed to a dumb-waiter which had been fixed so that he could sit on a small stool. They let him down into the kitchen, where they removed him and again transported him through the house to the library and his armchair. And he was there, a glass of sherry in one hand and a cigarette in the other, at five-thirty, when the guests began to arrive. They were limited now to those who knew him best and longest; they stayed, in groups of two or three, for almost half an hour. By eight o'clock it was time for him to return to his room by the means he had descended. No one who came to visit him in the course of the last few weeks will ever forget him. He demonstrated a unique, purely animal courage. After the first visit, nothing more was needed to reinforce the first shock caused by his devastating appearance—one quickly became aware of the greatness that it hid, and one felt strangely exalted, proud to be there, proud to be his friend, the friend of so courageous a man."

But courage was not enough. He died.

At his funeral on January 17, 1957, attended by hundreds, John Huston intoned the eulogy:

"... Bogie was happy at play and happy at love. From the beginning he had the greatest gift a man could have, talent. The whole world recognized it ... his life, although not particularly long, was richly lived ... he had obtained from life all that he wanted, and more. ..."

A woman sobbed.

Humphrey Bogart was dead, ashes in an urn. But he is survived by Duke Mantee, Turkey Morgan, Baby Face Martin, Roy Earle, Sam Spade, Rick, Dobbs, Dixon Steele, Charlie Allnut, Captain Queeg, Harry Dawes, Eddie Willis, and a host of others.

*Fade out to black.*


## Flashback I

Humphrey De Forest Bogart was born on Christmas Day in 1899, in a posh New York City clinic, and from the outset seemed miscast as the son of a prosperous surgeon, Belmont Bogart, and a noted magazine illustrator, Maud Humphrey. At the tender age of one he made his first public appearance, as the round and rosy model for one of his mother's children's portraits, captioned, "The Real Maud Humphrey Baby." Before long, at the age of five, he entered exclusive Trinity School. He was high-spirited and didn't seem to fit in with the other children of New York society.

His father had already mapped out Humphrey's future. After

Trinity School there would be Phillips Academy in Andover, Massachusetts, then Yale for premedical studies. Belmont wanted his son to follow in his footsteps and become a doctor.

But at Phillips, Humphrey was unruly and unmanageable, and was finally expelled for unceremoniously dumping a most unpopular assistant professor in a fountain.

Humphrey didn't want to return to his family home in New York. Years later he said: "Because I loved boats and water, I joined the Navy. The war was a big joke. Death? What does death mean to a kid of seventeen? The idea of death starts getting through to you when you're older—when you read obituaries about famous people whose accomplishments have touched you—and when people of your own generation die."

But the war did leave its mark. While serving as a helmsman aboard the troopship *Leviathan*, he scarred his lip. The rest of his tour of duty was uneventful, and before the war ended he served as a seaman on the destroyer *Santa Olivia*.

Back in New York he was more restless than ever. The thought of returning to school was distasteful. He felt that would offer him no release. His first peacetime job was inspecting tugs for the Pennsylvania Railroad. But this work palled within three months, and he switched his attentions to Wall Street. He discovered quickly that being a stockbroker held no attraction.

Years before, as a boy growing up in New York, he had become friendly with Bill Brady, Jr., son of the powerful theatrical producer William A. Brady. When no jobs presented themselves, he decided to have a talk with Mr. Brady. The conversation led to a job in the production end of the business, as stage manager and company manager. For fifty dollars a week Bogart supervised the business affairs of the company on the road.

"For three years, I worked for him... being fired and then rehired. Then one day he called me in. 'I'm going to make an actor out of you,' he said. 'Here's your part.' I had one line of dialogue. I gave a beautiful performance as the houseboy on opening night. As I carried out a tray of dishes, I dropped them and the audience howled."

In 1922 Bogart graduated to a slightly larger role in *Swifty*, starring Hale Hamilton and Frances Howard. "On opening night I got so scared I had to walk off the stage to get a glass of water, leaving Hale twiddling his thumbs. He was rather upset. So were the critics."

One critic who reviewed *Swifty* said: "The young man who embodied the young sprig is what is usually and mercifully described as inadequate."

But the public seemed to like Bogart. He appeared in a number of plays: *Meet The Wife, Nerves, Hell's Bells,* and *Cradle Snatchers,* usually playing the harmless collegiate with the slick hair, the spotless white flannels, and the tennis racket, who ran out onto the stage just before the curtain was run down. When there was no work as an actor, he was a company manager.

Then came more plays: *Saturday's Children, Skyrocket,* and *It's A Wise Child.*

"I decided to try the movies," Bogart recalled later. "I took dozens of tests, but my upper lip held me back. The final test was for the male lead in *The White Sister.* Another actor got the part—Ronald Colman—and I got my lip operated on by my dad, and almost immediately got a contract with Fox. They gave me a ticket and sent me to Hollywood for the lead in *The Man Who Came Back.* My pals Bobby Ames, Ken McKenna, and Charlie Farrell met me at the station, and we lunched together.

" 'It's swell to see you,' they said. 'What are you out for?' I told them I had come to play the lead in *The Man Who Came Back,* and they howled. They, too, had been brought out for the part. Farrell finally got it, and I went into a little thing called *A Devil With Women.*"

In his first film, Bogart played Victor McLaglen's irritating friend who managed to get the last laugh, whether in martial or amorous adventures. *The New York Times* film reviewer said: "This last is Humphrey Bogart, who makes his debut in talking pictures and gives an ingratiating performance. Mr. Bogart is both good-looking and intelligent."

Bogart was a man in a hurry. This obscure comedian was certain that his star was rising and that in no time at all he would be at the top.

But the roles he was to play in the next few years added little lustre to his star. *Up The River,* a prison farce, found him as a young lover, overshadowed by Spencer Tracy; in *Body And Soul,* as a young aviator, he was killed off early in the film; in Universal's *Bad Sister,* he played a heavy for the first time; then back with Victor McLaglen again in *Women Of All Nations.*

Bogart's next assignment, his last for Fox for more than twenty years, found him in a western, *A Holy Terror.* His billing improved considerably in *Love Affair* for Columbia, but the quality of the part left much to be desired. His next two films, *Big City Blues* and *Three On A Match*, found his billing slipping to the vanishing point, and he didn't rate a single line of comment in the reviews.

Discouraged, he returned to New York. His dreams of stardom had all but vanished, and he decided that the stage was his medium. But he was a little old for the juvenile roles he had been playing. The height of the Depression was upon New York, and it was one of the worst theatrical seasons in the history of Broadway. He appeared in a few plays and another movie, produced in New York, *Midnight*.

His friends were alarmed at his state of mind. He was on the verge of giving up, when he opened in *Invitation To A Murder* in 1934, a performance which Arthur Hopkins, the producer, saw and liked.

"It was Arthur Hopkins who discovered the criminal in me. I think he should get 10 per cent of everything I have earned since then!" Bogart avowed.

Hopkins thought that Bogart would be perfect for the role of Duke Mantee in the upcoming production of *The Petrified Forest*, but Robert E. Sherwood, Bogart's friend, and author of *The Petrified Forest*, didn't agree.

Bogart let his beard grow, lowered his voice slightly, developed an air of impenetrability. He *was* Duke Mantee, facing the accursed poet Allan Squire, facing his hostages, two millionaires and a girl, in a twilight world filled with dead trees. In the voice of Duke Mantee, a killer, he affirmed the right of the strongest and proclaimed as the sole human law that he who is strong shall rule the jungle.

The new Humphrey Bogart was born.

When Warner Brothers decided to bring *The Petrified Forest* to the screen in 1936, their first choice for the role of Duke Mantee was Edward G. Robinson, already famous for his gangster portrayals. But Robinson wanted a change from this typecasting and turned down the role. Bogart was still not considered for the role, until Leslie Howard, star of the play on Broadway and already cast for the film, refused to do the movie unless Bogart played Duke Mantee. Archie Mayo, Warner's director on the project, agreed, and Bogart emerged as a motion-picture force to be reckoned with.

Bogart began to get letters from young prisoners, young gangsters. For them he was the perfect model. He gained a following. Already he was being transformed into a legend. Hats were worn as he wore them. His melancholy was imitated. The Bogart myth had begun.

As a reward for his masterful characterization in *The Petrified Forest*, Bogart received a long-term contract with Warner Brothers. But in spite of the depth and scope Bogart brought to the role of Duke Mantee, he regularly played second-rate parts in second-rate films. He appeared in twenty-eight films in a period of five years and had a running battle with Jack Warner. Bogart was forced to submit to Warner's casting, but not without protest, casting in roles that almost never permitted him to express himself as he had done in *The Petrified Forest*.

During these years of controversy, Warner confined him to roles as villains and unsympathetic adventurers. He was offered only discontent, frustration. But somehow he kept his humor.

A newspaper story quoted Bogart calling Jack Warner a "creep." Warner was furious and called him.

"Come on, Jack, don't get angry. You don't even know what I mean by 'creep.'"

Warner bellowed: "I have a dictionary right here. Literally, 'creep' means a contemptible thing which crawls."

"That's a mistake, Jack. I spell it with a *k*. . . ."

During 1936 and 1937, Bogart made nine films for Warner. Few remember any of the films; the names hardly ring a bell: *Two Against The World, Bullets Or Ballots*, with Edward G. Robinson, *China Clipper, Isle Of Fury, The Great O'Malley, Black Legion, San Quentin, Marked Woman*, and *Kid Galahad*.

Bogart finally escaped the stereotyped roles being offered by Jack Warner in 1937 and 1938, with two films away from his parent studio. The first was *Dead End*, adapted by Lillian Hellman from Sidney Kingsley's hit play. Here, under the skillful direction of William Wyler, Bogart let emotion break through the mask of the gangster. For the first time since he created Duke Mantee in *The Petrified Forest*, Bogart was able to build a whole character. Here, as Martin, a product of the slums and a vicious killer, Bogart played one of his most brilliant scenes: his confrontation with his mother, a mother who despised him. Bogart giving a living, breathing characterization.

*Stand-In* for Walter Wanger and United Artists gave Bogart the chance at a real change of pace. For once he could look forward to attending a preview and not seeing himself hanged, electrocuted, or otherwise liquidated. He was a tough guy, a Hollywood production chief trying to save his studio, but this time on the side of the angels.

Then, after this brief respite, Bogart returned to the salt mines of the Warner Brothers lot. During 1938, 1939, and 1940, Bogart made seventeen films in quick succession: *Swing Your Lady*, a hillbilly farce which Bogart often called his worst film; *Men Are Such Fools;* another film with the Dead End Kids, *Crime School;* a psychological crime drama with Edward G. Robinson, *The Amazing Dr. Clitterhouse; Racket Busters; King of the Underworld; Angels With Dirty Faces*, with James Cagney; *You Can't Get Away With Murder; Dark Victory*, in which he played the Irish groom opposite Bette Davis's doomed heiress; a western, *The Oklahoma Kid*, with James Cagney; *The Return Of Dr. X*, in which Bogart played a vampire-doctor thirsting after fresh blood; a film about Prohibition, *The Roaring Twenties; Invisible Stripes*, with William Holden and George Raft; *Virginia City*, a Civil War drama; a comedy, *It All Came True; Brother Orchid*, with Edward G. Robinson; and finally, *They Drive By Night*, with George Raft, Ida Lupino, and Ann Sheridan.

These were not easy years for Bogart. Although his career was moving along, he still looked for and hoped for that one role, like Duke Mantee, which would catapult him to the top of his profession. It was only in 1941 that Warner Brothers offered him the chance he had been waiting for.

*High Sierra* was the real turning point in Bogart's film career. Here was the perfect marriage of talents: a brilliant screenplay by John Huston and W. R. Burnett, superb direction by Raoul Walsh, and, of course, Bogart. As an aging life-termer sprung from prison to pull one last job, Bogart *was* Mad Dog Roy Earle. Here was the perfect portrait of a man rushing headlong toward death, a man you are gradually allowed to hear tick but would not monkey with, a man you feel must be obeyed instinctively, a man you will never forget.

Bogart's next film, *The Wagons Roll At Night*, did little to enhance his growing reputation as an actor with deep understanding and feeling under a tough exterior. The character he played, Nick Coster, was one-dimensional.

But in October 1941, when *The Maltese Falcon* was released, Bogart's place in the top rank of Hollywood stars was assured. *The Maltese Falcon* was the directorial debut of John Huston, whose previous efforts had been limited to screenwriting, and his genius for drawing characterizations from actors was established. Bogart's portrayal of the tough, cynical private detective, Sam Spade, became a screen classic. It would serve as a model for hard-boiled private eyes for years to come.

*The Maltese Falcon* was a blockbuster for Bogart in every way. His popularity soared. No longer was he limited to playing "heavies." Here, after forty-two films, more than half of his career, Bogart had finally established himself. The directorial astuteness of Huston had forced people to understand that Bogart was a fine actor and much more than just a type.

Bogart's next two films, *All Through The Night* and *The Big Shot*, found him playing gangsters again, but with Huston again in *Across The Pacific*, Bogart showed that he could act.

*Casablanca*, in 1943, was both a major triumph and a breakthrough for Bogart. It was his first important romantic role since achieving stardom and added a new dimension to his screen personality. His love scenes with Ingrid Bergman showed that this man of violence was actually a tough guy with an Achilles heel. Bogart had a sense of melancholy about him which touched audiences and critics alike. For this performance, he was nominated for an Academy Award.

*Fade out to black.*

## Flashback II

"I'm a one-woman man," Bogart said once, "and I always have been." This was true in a manner of speaking—one woman at a time.

Bogart married four times.

While on tour as the stage manager of *Drifting* in 1924, Bogart met Helen Mencken, the star of the show. They soon became engaged, and in 1926 they were married. But Bogart was a man in a hurry, a man in search of himself and a career, a man with a driving ambition to succeed. The marriage lasted only a year and a half. "He placed," said Miss Mencken some time later, "more importance on his career than on his marriage."

Mary Phillips, convent bred, was his next wife. Even though she was a working actress, she couldn't keep up with Bogart. The night life was too much for her. She stayed in the background in silence, and after nearly ten years of marriage they were divorced.

During the filming of *Marked Woman* he met Mayo Methot, who was to become wife number three. She seemed to have the answer to the Bogart riddle: she would stay out with him as long as he wanted. Their life was a continual round of drinking and brawling.

"I married," she exploded with enthusiasm, "a man who conducts himself like a man. A man who doesn't only offer me security, but a certain excitement."

In Hollywood and across the nation they were known as The Battling Bogarts, and neither did anything to dispel this image. Whether at home or in the night clubs and restaurants they frequented, they almost always created a scene. One of Bogart's favorite pastimes was provoking Broderick Crawford in public. Great mock battles were fought in clubs all around Hollywood, and Mayo would always get into the act. She would play the part of referee and end the fight with shouts and hysterical cries. Mayo seemed to thrive on the combat. "She's an actress without work," Bogart explained, "and it's necessary for her to make scenes! So I give her the cue." At home, the war continued, in barrages of flying china and ash trays.

"My wife just missed me with an ash tray," he related to a telephone caller. "I don't know what's wrong with her aim lately."

And each and every battle was covered in the newspapers. There was hardly a day when there wasn't an item about them in the papers or on the wires.

When, in *Casablanca*, he met Ingrid Bergman, he never hid the fact that he felt she was the "only lady in Hollywood." This remark cut Mayo. "You're not, by any chance," questioned Mayo, "including me, your wife, are you?"

Bogart replied characteristically: "If the shoe fits, dear..."

Mayo was jealous, and at times she was sure that Bogart was playing around. She went so far as to have him followed by a private investigator.

Occasionally they came to blows in public.

In 1944, Bogart, Mayo, Peter Lorre, and a number of other Hollywood celebrities went overseas to entertain the American troops, and his running battle with Mayo was every bit as savage as any fighting they saw in North Africa. In Tunisia they got into a brawl and broke up all the furniture in their room. On their return to the United States Bogart calmly announced that they had been thrown out of Africa—and Italy.

Bogart's reputation as a two-fisted, hard-drinking tough guy was growing, and this added to his popularity. But the image of the tough guy was continually getting him into trouble. It seemed that every time he went into a restaurant someone would challenge him to see whether or not he was as tough as his last screen role. And Mayo egged him on. Once a man came over to him and mussed his hair. Mayo shouted: "Hit him!" Bogart knocked him down and had to leave the premises. The Battling Bogarts were banned from a number of the best Hollywood night clubs.

They even battled about politics. During the campaign in 1944, Bogart supported Roosevelt, Mayo stumped for Dewey. Finally, Bogart moved out and they were divorced. He had already met the woman that would be his fourth wife.

Howard Hawks had already decided that Bogart would play Harry Morgan in *To Have And Have Not*. The character of the rugged sea dog who would run his boat to hell and back with no questions asked would be perfect for him. But casting the leading lady was more difficult.

Hawks was looking for a new face to play opposite Bogart and, on the suggestion of his wife, tested Lauren Bacall, a long-stemmed fashion model. She not only won the role, but Bogart as well. During the filming of *To Have And Have Not*, Bogart helped the youngster. And when she said: "If you want anything, all you have to do is whistle," Bogart fell.

On May 21, 1945, Bogart married Bacall, and no one in Hollywood gave the marriage a chance. He was more than twice her age and already an established star; she was a cover-girl starlet. But they were all wrong. The marriage worked. Bogart once explained why Betty had married him:

"Career girls especially don't want to go through the struggle of marrying a young man who's searching for a job. That's what Betty told me before we got married. She liked the idea of moving into an established home. Most girls today aren't the covered-wagon type. They prefer older husbands."

Bogart loved the sea, and with Betty he was able to relax aboard their yacht, *Santana*. "Next to an actor," he used to say, "I'd rather be a sailor than anything. The sea," he affirmed, "is the only place where man can still experience the feeling of being free."

He dressed in a simple manner. He preferred rough cloth to fancy suits. He enjoyed Betty's company.

But Bogart, as always, treated the Hollywood of the publicity man and the artificial build-up with disdain. He thoroughly enjoyed being different. "In Hollywood I am what is called anti-social," Bogart once said with a smile. "People do not invite me to their homes because they are afraid I might say the wrong thing to Louis B. Mayer, Darryl Zanuck, or Jack Warner, which I probably would."

Bogart was a living, breathing human being. He was never impressed by the newspaper stories that carried items about his wealth: his home worth $160,000; his two Jaguars, a Mark VII for Betty and an XK 120 for himself; his $55,000 yacht. He was not obsessed by status, and he despised this obsession in others.

In 1949, when Betty gave birth to his first child, he said: "She is my swan song. She is everything that I ever wanted, and now, Stephen, my son, completes the picture." When his daughter, Leslie, was born in 1952, the picture *was* complete.

Lauren Bacall, born Betty Joan Persky, had discovered something that no one else had:

"I married an old-fashioned man—eighteenth century. He's a prude. This surprises you. These are not the terms in which you think of him. But let me tell you something. Bogie, because he is not a secure man, is a very deceptive man."

*Fade out to black.*

## Fade In

Ten films over the span of five years bridged the gap between great performances, between *Casablanca* and *The Treasure Of The Sierra Madre*. It was almost as if Bogart were waiting for John Huston to return from his tour of duty in World War II to give him another opportunity to assert himself.

*Action In The North Atlantic*, with Bogart as a first mate aboard a transport ship, *Thank Your Lucky Stars*, and *Sahara*, the story of a wayward tank in the desert, were all released in 1943.

In 1944, he made *Passage To Marseille*, and in 1945, he played a wife-murderer in a psychological drama, *Conflict*.

Warner Brothers hit a box-office bonanza when they teamed Bogart with newcomer Lauren Bacall in *To Have And Have Not*, and continued to ride this success with *The Big Sleep* and *Dark Passage*.

*The Two Mrs. Carrolls* and *Dead Reckoning*, both released in

1947, kept Bogart in *Motion Picture Herald*'s list of top money-making stars in Hollywood. In 1947 he made over $400,000.

However, it was in his next film, again under the expert and searching direction of John Huston, that Bogart reached another plateau in his acting career. *The Treasure Of The Sierra Madre* proved beyond a doubt that he could, in the right role, achieve a performance of lasting greatness.

As Dobbs, Bogart appeared as an unshaven, gross, shifty-eyed wanderer in Mexico. Even for Bogart, who never balked at the realistic approach, it was an extraordinarily unattractive character. Bogart brought Dobbs to life on the screen, a man consumed by passion for gold who, in the end, loses everything. He was, quite simply, superb.

Huston and Bogart continued their collaboration in *Key Largo*, in which Bogart, as a disillusioned ex-soldier, learned that good men must make a commitment in order to prevent evil.

Bogart himself, in 1947, had been willing to make a commitment. He took part in a march to Washington to protest the activities of the House Un-American Activities Committee, and for his trouble he was labeled a "pinko" by many.

Bogart, like most experienced actors, felt the urge to go into business for himself. He set up his own production company, Santana Productions, named after his yacht. His first production was *Knock On Any Door*, in which he played an attorney, Andrew Morton, a graduate of Skid Row who understands the violence in his young client. While the picture was not wholly satisfying, it was an interesting film with a point of view.

Within the next two years his company produced three other films: *Tokyo Joe*, *In A Lonely Place*, and *Sirocco*. The only one worthy of discussion was *In A Lonely Place*.

Playing a violent, quick-tempered Hollywood movie writer, Bogart loomed large on the screen and moved flawlessly through the script, which was almost as flinty as the actor himself. Bogart did not psychoanalyze the character of Dixon Steele. He lived him. During this same time he appeared in his last two films for Warner Brothers, *Chain Lightning* and *The Enforcer*, which ended his association with the studio that had begun in 1932.

"I'm absolutely against competition in the arts. Let everyone play the same role and then you've got a measure for selecting. How can you truly compare one man's melancholy Dane with another's baby-sitter?"

Bogart made this statement in 1949 when he asserted that he would never go near an Oscar presentation. Bogart went so far as to establish a mock award for the best performance in a film by an animal, making sure that the bit of satire received full notice in the press. Yet, when he was nominated for his performance in *The African Queen*, and the night of the presentations rolled around, he was more nervous than anyone. As the other nominees were read: Marlon Brando for *A Streetcar Named Desire;* Fredric March for *Death Of A Salesman;* Arthur Kennedy for *Bright Victory;* and Montgomery Clift for *A Place In The Sun*, Bogart got out of his seat and paced.

It was Bogart, in his sixty-fifth film, playing the part of a dissolute riverboat captain, who walked off with the honor.

John Huston, as he had in *The Maltese Falcon* and *The Treasure Of The Sierra Madre*, gave Bogart the chance to reach the height of his art. Bogart and the character he was playing became intertwined as a single being under Huston's direction. Charlie, an old bushman, alone and wild, stinking of gin, gnashing his teeth, had returned to the primitive. Into this life came a puritanical old maid, Rose. Charlie was compelled to action by her and finally was led to the road of tenderness and love so long forgotten. Swimming to the bank of the river with Rose, Charlie Allnut burst into laughter, and it seemed as if it were Bogart himself who laughed.

Bogart had created a characterization that must be rated as superb. There was not even a trace of his former tough personality in Charlie Allnut. It was a completely new kind of role.

When Bogart, Hepburn, Huston, and a large crew, plus Betty, had gone to Africa for location work on the film, Bogart had been miserable. He hated the jungle, the heat, and the insects. "I found a way to beat the bugs," he stated. "I burn 'em, kill 'em. All I do is drink three double scotches a day."

Bogart wasn't particularly fond of Katharine Hepburn, his co-star. "I couldn't stand her for the first two weeks. She talks to you like you were a microphone. She doesn't want any answers." But by the end of the filming they had become friends.

This was the third time that Bogart had been nominated for the Best Actor laurels: first as Rick in *Casablanca;* then as Dobbs in *The Treasure Of The Sierra Madre;* and now as Charlie Allnut.

After his victory, he remarked in true Bogartian style: "I'm going out to get loaded."

After the completion of *The African Queen*, Bogart seemed to put more and more of himself into each film and into each role that he played. In the ten films which followed *The African Queen*, he assumed ten aliases, and with the help of his directors, Richard Brooks, John Huston, Edward Dmytryk, Billy Wilder, Joseph L. Mankiewicz, Michael Curtiz, William Wilder, and Mark Robson, his genius was confirmed.

*Alias Ed Hutcheson in* Deadline-U.S.A.

As the crusading editor, Bogart fought against the world of crime, a world that he had so often portrayed in his earlier films. Bogart's intelligence and will shone through the character. Hutcheson in the film, like Bogart in reality, learned that good does not always triumph, that everything is not really for the best in this best of all possible worlds.

*Alias Jed Webbe in* Battle Circus

Richard Brooks's direction of this film permitted Bogart to reveal an important facet of his true personality. Bogart, as Webbe, an Army major in the Korean War, denounced the hero whose violence he had glorified. As he drank his whiskey, he consumed not only the alcohol, but the things which he might love. The bitterness became hidden and the brutality became dulled as he let himself be penetrated by tenderness. Brooks once said about his films: "I depict in general a human being who is opposed to the time in which he lives and the fight which he carries on in order to free himself of the fetters of the past, to blossom and to continue to grow. The heroes of my films are always searching for some means of expressing themselves fully." It was almost as if he had been talking about Bogart.

*Alias Billy Dannreuther in* Beat The Devil

A Hollywood wit once said: "The trouble with Bogart is that he thinks he's Bogart." The remark was meant invidiously, but, in Billy Dannreuther, Bogart found part of himself at least. The cynicism which turned to scepticism, that certain offhandedness, accompanied by intelligence and shrewdness, were a part of both Dannreuther and Bogart. For this film, Bogart was teamed with his friend and mentor, John Huston, for the last time.

*Alias Captain Queeg in* The Caine Mutiny

Bogart's portrait of Captain Queeg was full, rich, and complete: a man of courage who was broken by the ordeals in life that he met but failed to conquer. This role came close to earning Bogart his second Oscar. He was acclaimed as the Best Actor by the judges of the Venice Film Festival, in this his most violent film. Bogart showed a man haunted by interior demons, who completely falls to pieces and is destroyed by his own weakness. His success in this film, under the direction of Edward Dmytryk, was almost absolute, a role that was so full of truth that it reached the audience and exhausted it with its very intensity.

*Alias Linus Larrabee in* Sabrina

Billy Wilder led Bogart into one of his very rare comedy appearances, as businessman Linus Larrabee who falls unexpectedly under the charms of Audrey Hepburn. Wilder allowed Bogart to play an anti-Bogart role which fascinated Bogart.

*Alias Harry Dawes in* The Barefoot Contessa

Bogart often said: "Pick a fine director, and you can't lose." One of his best choices was Joseph L. Mankiewicz, with whom he worked in *The Barefoot Contessa*. Never before had Bogart played a character that was so much like himself—a man who regarded the world from the outside, a passer-by whose cynicism and profound tenderness touches each of us. When we see the film we are looking at Bogart, or Dawes, a face full of melancholy and sadness.

*Alias Joseph in* We're No Angels

Bogart was a man that presented to the world a hard exterior, but all who knew him understood that this was merely a public image. His friends knew that under this hard exterior there was a man with understanding and sympathy, a man with courage and deep feeling. As Joseph, a Devil's Island escapee, a forger and a swindler *par excellence*, who consorts with a strangler and a safecracker, Bogart showed this face to the public. Here was the tough guy with a heart who tried not to show his feelings.

*Alias Glenn Griffin in* The Desperate Hours

Bogart and Glenn Griffin were brothers under the skin: they both were about to face death. As Griffin, Bogart wore the mask of the gangster for the last time. As played by Bogart, Griffin was the most vicious, intelligent criminal ever put on film. In this role Bogart was so forceful, impressive, and brilliant that it was a fitting climax to a career which found its way to prominence through playing Duke Mantee. For Griffin is Duke Mantee at the age of fifty, with graying hair and tired heart. And it was William Wyler, the man who gave Bogart the opportunity to show sensitivity eighteen years earlier in *Dead End*, who at the end of Bogart's career gave him the chance to come full cycle, from Duke Mantee to Duke Mantee.

*Alias Jim Carmody in* The Left Hand Of God

As Carmody, an unscrupulous American flyer who turns adven-

26

turer after the war to become the leader of a Chinese warlord's nondescript army, Bogart portrayed a man of surface roughness but with innate dignity. Time and again Bogart replayed this theme, which seemed to be the central theme of his life. Lauren Bacall often attributed this facet of his character to the fact that he was really insecure, and this insecurity is portrayed with brilliance in this role.

*Alias Eddie Willis in* The Harder They Fall

Bogart appeared on the screen for the last time as he actually was, without make-up, and with his face showing the signs of death that would soon take him. Bogart was superb as the decent man sucked into a filthy racket by his need for money, trying to ease his conscience with the balm of cash, and failing in his effort to sell himself out. His mounting fury against the forces of evil was in proportion to the discovery of the callousness surrounding him. Bogart's blunt, driving technique as an actor and the scarcely repressed violence he brought to the screen were both perfectly fitted to the role.

## And So The Last Film Had Been Made.

It remains that Humphrey Bogart was one of the most paradoxical screen personalities in the recent annals of Hollywood. Often he deflated the publicity balloons that so many stars found necessary to keep aloft, and yet he was one of the greatest box-office attractions for more than twenty years.

He had a large, seemingly permanent following among the mass audience, although he hated mass activities.

"I am a professional," he would say fiercely. "I have a respect for my profession."

John Huston put it best:

"Over the years he had become more and more conscious of the dignity of his profession: Actor, not Star. He never took himself too seriously, but he took his work with enormous seriousness. He considered the slightly garish image of Bogart the star with amused cynicism; but he held Bogart the actor in high esteem."

And finally:

"Those who did not know him well, who never worked with him, who did not belong to the small group of his intimate friends, have a completely different idea of the man who had these rare gifts.

"He is absolutely irreplaceable. There will never be another one like him."

# A Devil With Women

Jerry Maxton, soldier of fortune, is stranded in a small Central American country. He is hired by the government of the banana republic to lend his sword and swagger to suppress a group of armed bandits and guerillas who have been terrorizing the country.

With him is a brash, irritating young man, Tom Standish, who somehow manages to get the last laugh, romantically and militarily, in almost every situation.

Rosita proves to be a great help. She lures the bandits into her house, one by one, whereupon Jerry removes them from active combat with a short jolt to the chin.

Two coy senoritas are almost their undoing. They lure Jerry and Standish into the camp of the enemy where they are brought face to face with the bandit chief. Jerry and Standish are condemned to die by firing squad, but with the help of Rosita, they narrowly escape.

Jerry and Standish become fast friends.

Directed by Irving Cummings. Screenplay and dialogue by Dudley Nichols and Henry M. Johnson. From the novel *Dust And Sun* by Clement Ripley. Release date, November 1930. A Fox Film.

| | |
|---|---|
| Jerry Maxton | *Victor McLaglen* |
| Rosita | *Mona Maris* |
| Tom Standish | *Humphrey Bogart* |
| Bandit Chief | *Michael Vavitch* |

With: *Luana Alcaniz, John St. Polis, Mona Rico, Joe De La Cruz.*

*With Mona Maris*

# Up The River

Directed by John Ford. Story by Maurine Watkins. Release date, October 1930. A Fox Film.

| | |
|---|---|
| St. Louis | *Spencer Tracy* |
| Judy | *Claire Luce* |
| Dannemora Dan | *Warren Hymer* |
| Steve | *Humphrey Bogart* |
| Pop | *William Collier, Sr.* |
| The Warden's Daughter | *Joan Lawes* |
| Jessup | *George MacFarlane* |
| Morris | *Gaylord Pendleton* |
| Edith La Verne | *Sharon Lynn* |
| Sophie | *Noel Francis* |
| Kit | *Goodee Montgomer* |
| Slim and Klem | *Black and Blue* |

St. Louis and Dannemora Dan are convicts. Following an examination to determine the mental equipment of the inmates, Dan appears with a paper in his hand. He asks what *m-o-r-o-n* spells and when he is told, he is none the wiser.

Pop, a veteran felon, has one ambition after spending forty years within the gray walls. He wants the prison baseball team to triumph over the team of a rival prison.

The team has as its mascot a donkey painted with zebra-like stripes. The rival team turns up in an armored prison wagon from which several keepers with guns appear. The players on the bench are handcuffed until they are called upon to play.

St. Louis is a good pitcher, but Pop's chances are doomed when St. Louis and Dan escape from jail. They go to help Steve, an ex-convict.

Steve had been serving a term for "accidental manslaughter." He met Judy, a victim of a swindler, who was conveniently located in the women's wing of the penitentiary. All through his prison term Steve had succeeded in fooling his family and friends. They believed that he was in China. But when he'd served his sentence, Forsby, the rogue who had put Judy behind bars, threatens to expose him if he does not help him in a nefarious plan.

St. Louis and Dannemora Dan take care of Forsby and return to prison in time for St. Louis to pitch for the team.

*With
Claire
Luce*

*With
Spencer
Tracy*

# Body And Soul

Several American flyers are attached to a Royal Air Force squadron in France. Among them are Mal Andrews, Jim Watson, and Tap Johnson. Watson was married just a few days before he sailed, but has since picked up a girl in Europe.

General Trafford-Jones lectures the squadron on not getting results. His harangue is anything but tactful. He wants an enemy balloon brought down. Jim Watson is killed while attempting this feat. Eventually Mal Andrews downs the balloon.

Andrews feels that it is necessary for him to return the watch and letters which Watson had received from a girl called Pom-Pom. A newspaper ad finally brings a girl to the English inn where Andrews is spending leave. He assumes that she is·Pom-Pom. He tells her of Watson's death. Soon Andrews and Pom-Pom become interested in each other. She doesn't tell him that she isn't Pom-Pom.

Andrews is an innocent. He sprays perfume on himself and gargles with brandy to make his comrades think that he has spent a riotous evening. In a restaurant in London, he pours a glass of wine and slyly dumps the wine out, and, to his surprise, he learns that Pom-Pom has been doing likewise.

In the meantime, the intelligence service accuses Pom-Pom of being a spy with Andrews as her accomplice. The circumstances seem stacked against them. Andrews is certain that he has been double-crossed.

Ordered confined to his quarters, Andrews steals a British plane and flies to London, determined to shoot the girl who has blasted both his ideals and his war record at the same time.

When he arrives, he discovers that the girl he thought was Pom-Pom is in reality Carla, Watson's widow. The real Pom-Pom is someone else altogether.

Directed by Alfred Santell. Based on the play *Squadrons*. Release date, February 1931. Produced by the Fox Film Corporation.

| | |
|---|---|
| Mal Andrews | *Charles Farrell* |
| Carla | *Elissa Landi* |
| Jim Watson | *Humphrey Bogart* |
| Alice Lester | *Myrna Loy* |
| Tap Johnson | *Donald Dillaway* |
| Major Burke | *Crauford Kent* |
| Major Knowls | *Pat Somerset* |
| General Trafford-Jones | *Ian MacLaren* |
| Lieutenant Meggs | *Dennis d'Auburn* |
| Zane | *Douglas Dray* |
| Young | *Harold Kinney* |
| Sam Douglas | *Bruce Warren* |

# Bad Sister

Directed by Hobart Henley. Based on Booth Tarkington's story, *The Flirt*. Release date, March 1931. A Universal Picture.

| | |
|---|---|
| Dick Lindle | *Conrad Nagel* |
| Marianne | *Sidney Fox* |
| Laura | *Bette Davis* |
| Minnie | *Zasu Pitts* |
| Sam | *Slim Summerville* |
| Mr. Madison | *Charles Winninger* |
| Mrs. Madison | *Emma Dunn* |
| Valentine Corliss | *Humphrey Bogart* |
| Wade Trumbull | *Bert Roach* |
| Hedrick Madison | *David Durand* |

Marianne and Laura Madison are sisters living in a small Midwestern town. The tragedy of the Madison household is that Marianne is constantly pursued by all the young blades of the community, while Laura, the sad-faced Cinderella of the family, is left alone with her knitting most of the time.

In her room at night, Laura is fond of confiding to her diary that she loves a struggling young physician, Dr. Dick Lindley. As for Dick, he is smitten with a hopeless affection for her more colorful sister.

Marianne is dissatisfied with her life in the small town, with its humdrum existence. She falls ready victim to Mr. Valentine Corliss, who arrives in town with plans for a mythical factory which needs a little backing.

She forges her father's signature to a letter endorsing the factory and elopes with the glib young man. He leaves her stranded in their hotel the next morning.

Marianne returns home to find that Laura is engaged to Dr. Lindley, and as a solution for her problems, Marianne marries Wade Trumbull, a wealthy nitwit for whom she has previously felt only an amused contempt.

*With Conrad Nagel and Sidney Fox*

*With Sidney Fox*

*With Edmund Lowe and Victor McLaglen*

Flagg and Quirt, the characters so popular in *What Price Glory*, are at it again, this time *after* the war. In Brooklyn, Flagg is a recruiting officer for the Marines, and Quirt operates a Turkish bath for women. The place is raided. Flagg agrees to save Quirt from the police, if Quirt will rejoin the Marines. Since he has no choice, he does.

From Brooklyn Flagg and Quirt travel with Olsen, another Marine buddy, on a good-will tour to Sweden, where, in the land of snow and ice, they find the warm and alluring Elsa, a café entertainer. Here they celebrate Christmas by trying to win Elsa's affections. But they also meet Elsa's boy friend, a giant named Olaf. In a rage, Olaf throws the three Marines through a wall and subsequently tears down the entire building. They leave town.

In the course of time the three adventurers find themselves in Turkey. Here they learn that Elsa has become the favorite wife in the harem of much-married Prince Hassan.

The lads finally manage to sneak into the harem with Olsen, who finds that the many wives are anxious to hear his stories.

Again Flagg and Quirt both make a play for Elsa, but are interrupted in the *amour* when Prince Hassan shows up unexpectedly. As a result they all flee from the palace for the final fade-out.

Directed by Raoul Walsh. Release date, May 1931. A Fox Film.

| | |
|---|---|
| Sergeant Flagg | *Victor McLaglen* |
| Sergeant Quirt | *Edmund Lowe* |
| Elsa | *Greta Nissen* |
| Olsen | *El Brendel* |
| Fifi | *Fifi D'Orsay* |
| Pee Wee | *Marjorie White* |
| Captain of Marines | *T. Roy Barnes* |
| Prince Hassan | *Bela Lugosi* |
| Stone | *Humphrey Bogart* |
| Kiki | *Joyce Compton* |
| Izzie | *Jesse De Vorska* |
| Leon | *Charles Judels* |

# A Holy Terror

Directed by Irving Cummings. Based on Max Brand's story, *Trailin'*. Release date, July 1931. A Fox Film.

| | |
|---|---|
| Tony Bard | *George O'Brien* |
| Jerry Foster | *Sally Eilers* |
| Kitty Carroll | *Rita La Roy* |
| Steve Nash | *Humphrey Bogart* |
| William Drew | *James Kirkwood* |
| Butch Morgan | *Stanley Fields* |
| Thomas Woodbury | *Robert Warwick* |
| Tom Hedges | *Richard Tucker* |
| Jim Lawler | *Earl Pingree* |

Mr. Bard dies under mysterious circumstances. Tony, his son, a polo-playing millionaire, looks through his father's papers and discovers that the family name had not always been Bard. He also finds the name William Drew. Tony suspects that Mr. Drew, a rancher out West, knows a good deal about the mysterious death. Tony decides to find William Drew, to find the true story of his father.

Flying West, Tony loses control of his plane and crashes into Jerry Foster's bathtub.

The foreman of the ranch, Steve Nash, has a grievance against Tony as soon as he arrives. Steve is in love with Jerry and doesn't want Tony to get in his way.

Drew orders Steve and ranch hand Butch Morgan to bring Tony to him unharmed and unarmed. Tony escapes from the two men as they are trying to bring him in. He rides to the ranch himself for a showdown with Drew. Butch steps into the picture and attempts to shoot Tony, but Drew steps in front of the bullet and is wounded in the shoulder.

Then the story is told: Drew is really Tony's father. He had gone East for a reckoning with the man who had stolen his wife and child many years before. The gun which killed the supposed father had gone off accidentally during a scuffle.

*With Sally Eilers (above) and George O'Brien (below)*

# Love Affair

Jim Leonard is the instructor when Carol Owen, an heiress, decides to take flying lessons. They fall rather thoroughly in love in the course of the instruction, and it all seems perfectly simple. But he happens to be an inventor with a newly designed motor very much on his mind, and as inventors so often are, he is poor. He feels that he would be entirely out of place among the Owens millions and tells Carol how he feels.

Suddenly and unexpectedly, Carol finds herself in a decidedly penniless situation, which places them on even terms. She finds out about her situation only when she is about to invest in Jim's motor. Making the sacrifice, she offers to marry Mr. Hardy, a wealthy broker, in order to secure backing for Jim.

Jim learns of the plan, calls off the deal with Mr. Hardy, and succeeds in obtaining the backing of his former employer. Carol cancels her engagement to Mr. Hardy when she learns that he has bought a controlling interest in the motor company. Jim returns to his old job as a mechanic.

Carol tries to commit suicide, flying a plane by herself, but Jim reaches the plane just in time to save her.

Directed by Thornton Freeland. Adaptation and dialogue by Jo Swerling. Based on a story by Ursulla Parrott. Release date, March 1932. A Columbia Picture.

| | |
|---|---|
| Carol Owen | *Dorothy Mackaill* |
| Jim Leonard | *Humphrey Bogart* |
| Gilligan | *Jack Kennedy* |
| Felice | *Barbara Leonard* |
| Linda Lee | *Astrid Allwyn* |
| Georgie | *Bradley Page* |
| Kibbee | *Halliwell Hobbes* |
| Mr. Hardy | *Hale Hamilton* |
| Antone | *Harold Minjir* |

# Big City Blues

Directed by Mervyn Le Roy. From an un-produced play by Ward Morehouse. Release date, September 1932. A Warner Brothers Picture.

| | |
|---|---|
| Vida | Joan Blondell |
| Bud Reeves | Eric Linden |
| Faun | Inez Courtney |
| Jo-Jo | Evalyn Knapp |
| Hummel | Guy Kibbee |
| Sully | Lyle Talbot |
| Agnes | Gloria Shea |
| Gibbony | Walter Catlett |
| Serena | Jobyna Howland |
| Adkins | Humphrey Bogart |
| Jackie | Josephine Dunn |
| Station Agent | Grant Mitchell |
| Quilkin | Thomas Jackson |
| Stackhouse | Ned Sparks |
| Lorna | Sheila Terry |
| Red | Tom Dugan |
| Mabel | Betty Gillette |
| Baggage Master | Edward McWade |

Bud Reeves, a country boy from Hoopersville, Indiana, inherits over a thousand dollars and decides to come to New York City. When he gets to New York he meets his cousin, Gibbony. Gibbony welcomes him because he is continually broke and he believes that he can get some money from his country cousin.

Gibbony convinces Bud to throw a big party in his hotel room, a party which ends abruptly when a young girl is killed with a bottle thrown by a drunk.

Everybody flees, including Bud and a chorus girl, Vida, whom he met at the party. They are both arrested, however, and things look bad for Bud and Vida, because the murder took place in his hotel room. They are finally cleared when the real culprit is identified by the hotel detective. The real murderer is found hanging in a linen closet, a suicide.

Bud, with Vida, visits a gambling casino. He starts with a tremendous pile of chips, but before long has lost everything.

Bud returns to Hoopersville to work hard to save enough money to return to Manhattan and settle down with Vida as his wife.

*With Inez Courtney, Walter Catlett, Lyle Talbot, Sheila Terry, Ned Sparks, and Josephine Dunn*

# Three On A Match

Three classmates, Mary Keaton, Vivian Revere, and Ruth West-cott, meet ten years after graduation. Vivian is married and has a son, Junior; Ruth is a stenographer; and Mary, after time in a reformatory, is a show girl.

Vivian is bored with her wealthy husband, Kirkwood, and falls in love with Mike Loftus, a petty racketeer. She leaves Kirkwood to live with Mike.

Mary tries to talk sense into Vivian, but she won't listen to any advice. Kirkwood divorces her and gets custody of Junior. After a time he falls in love with Mary, and they are married.

Vivian and Mike are broke, and Mike is in trouble with Ace, a racket boss, because of a bad check he has issued. He forces Vivian to beg Mary for money. But it is not enough to clear him. As a last resort he tries to blackmail Kirkwood with a threat to reveal the fact that Mary had been in reform school. Failing in this, he kidnaps Junior and holds him for $2,000 ransom. Ace and his gang have heard of it and decide to take over the job and play for much higher stakes. Vivian, who has gone down the trail of drink and dope, is rendered helpless in her efforts to keep her child from coming to harm, and is as much a prisoner as Junior.

There is an intense search by the police for Junior and the kidnappers, but with no result. Seeing that they cannot collect, the gang decides to get rid of the child. Mike is delegated to do the dirty work. He is killed when he refuses.

Racked with desire for liquor and drugs, Vivian is still able to scheme for her child's safety. With a lipstick she writes the location of the kidnappers' apartment on the nightgown she is wearing. Caught in the act, she hurls herself from the apartment window. The police find her dying on the pavement below, and the message on her nightgown.

The gang is captured, the child returned to Kirkwood, and they all forgive Vivian.

Directed by Mervyn Le Roy. Story by Kubec Glasmon and John Bright. Release date, October 1932. A Warner Brothers-First National Picture.

| | |
|---|---|
| Mary Keaton | *Joan Blondell* |
| Henry Kirkwood | *Warren William* |
| Vivian Revere | *Ann Dvorak* |
| Ruth Westcott | *Bette Davis* |
| School Principal | *Grant Mitchell* |
| Michael Loftus | *Lyle Talbot* |
| Naomi | *Sheila Terry* |
| Mrs. Black | *Glenda Farrell* |
| Mrs. Keaton | *Clara Blandick* |
| Junior | *Buster Phelps* |
| Ace | *Humphrey Bogart* |
| Henchman | *Allen Jenkins* |
| Bilkerson | *John Marston* |
| Linda | *Patricia Ellis* |
| Defense Attorney | *Hale Hamilton* |

*With Allen Jenkins, Ann Dvorak, and Buster Phelps*

# Midnight

Directed by Chester Erskine. An adaptation of the play by Claire and Paul Sifton. Release date, January 1934. A Universal Picture.

| | |
|---|---|
| Stella Weldon | *Sidney Fox* |
| Edward Weldon | *O.P. Heggie* |
| Nolan | *Henry Hull* |
| Mrs. Weldon | *Margaret Wycherly* |
| Joe Biggers | *Lynne Overman* |
| Ada Biggers | *Katherine Wilson* |
| Arthur Weldon | *Richard Whorf* |
| Garboni | *Humphrey Bogart* |
| Henry McGrath | *Granville Bates* |
| Elizabeth McGrath | *Cora Witherspoon* |
| District Attorney Plunkett | *Moffat Johnson* |
| Mr. Ingersoll | *Henry O'Neill* |
| Ethel Saxon | *Helen Flint* |

In a courtroom, a woman is being tried for murder. Since the murder could be considered a crime of passion, it looks very much as if she will be acquitted.

Edward Weldon, the foreman of the jury, asks a question. "Did you take his money after you killed him?" She says, "Yes," and that answer convicts her.

Edward Weldon is generally accused of having been to blame for sentencing the woman to death in the electric chair. His life is made miserable by reporters and others.

On the very night of the execution, Weldon is plagued by reporters into repeating his stand: "The woman committed murder; she must pay the price."

Then, at midnight, just as the woman he sentenced is going to the chair, the horror of the situation is intensified when his own daughter murders her lover, who has betrayed her.

Weldon, sticking to his principles, swears that his own daughter must also pay the penalty. A young reporter, however, convinces the district attorney not to prosecute. The crime is concealed, and the young girl is convinced that she only *imagined* the murder.

48

# The Petrified Forest

Alan Squier, who eight years before had published a brilliant first novel, suddenly finds that his wealthy wife wants to marry another man. The knowledge makes him realize that for eight years he has been a parasite, that he has done nothing, has not even lived. He leaves his wife and goes forth seeking to find some reason for living.

His search brings him to the Maple Service Station, in the barren desert, fifteen miles from the Petrified Forest. In the station live Jason Maple and his father, Gramps, who has thousands of dollars in Liberty Bonds but will not give the money to his family. He also finds Gabby, who wants to go to France where she was born, and Boze Hertzlinger, a 100-per-cent American college boy who has a deep passion for Gabby.

On the day Squier arrives at the service station, Duke Mantee and his gang have massacred six persons in Oklahoma and are headed for the Petrified Forest. Gabby falls in love with Squier the moment she meets him. But he will not stay, and when Mrs. Chisholm and her husband come in their Rolls-Royce, he continues on his way with them.

But Mantee and his men stop them, steal their car, and head for the service station. Squier goes back to warn Gabby and finds that the gang has possession of the place. The Chisholms come back.

Boze, in an effort to show off, seizes a gun, but he is shot in the hand. Then Squier, who has learned of Gabby's desire to get away, decides to be noble, to give his life some meaning after all. He signs over his $5,000 insurance policy to Gabby, and, without her knowledge, he makes a bargain with Mantee for the gangster to kill him.

A sheriff's posse comes looking for Mantee and his gang. There is a fierce battle. Mantee uses Chisholm as a shield and starts for the car, but he comes back to fulfill his bargain. He shoots Squier and then makes his getaway. Squier dies in Gabby's arms.

Directed by Archie L. Mayo. Screenplay by Charles Kenyon and Delmar Daves. From the play by Robert Emmet Sherwood. Release date, February 1936. A Warner Brothers Picture.

| | |
|---|---|
| Alan Squier | *Leslie Howard* |
| Gabrielle Maple | *Bette Davis* |
| Mrs. Chisholm | *Genevieve Tobin* |
| Boze Hertzlinger | *Dick Foran* |
| Duke Mantee | *Humphrey Bogart* |
| Jackie | *Joseph Sawyer* |
| Jason Maple | *Porter Hall* |
| Gramps Maple | *Charley Grapewin* |
| Mr. Chisholm | *Paul Harvey* |
| Lineman | *Eddie Acuff* |
| Ruby | *Adrian Morris* |
| Paula | *Nina Campana* |
| Slim | *Slim Thompson* |
| Joseph | *John Alexander* |

# Two Against The World

Directed by William McGann. Screenplay by
Michel Jacoby. From an idea by Louis
Weitzenkorn. Release date, July 1936.
A Warner Brothers-First National Picture.

| | |
|---|---|
| Sherry Scott | *Humphrey Bogart* |
| Alma Ross | *Beverly Roberts* |
| Edith Carstairs | *Linda Perry* |
| William Sims, Jr. | *Carlyle Moore, Jr.* |
| Jim Carstairs | *Henry O'Neill* |
| Martha Carstairs | *Helen MacKellar* |
| Cora Latimer | *Claire Dodd* |
| Tippy Mantus | *Hobart Cavanaugh* |
| Martin Leavenworth | *Harry Hayden* |
| Bertram C. Reynolds | *Robert Middlemas* |
| Mr. Banning | *Clay Clement* |
| Malcolm Sims | *Douglas Wood* |
| Mrs. Marion Sims | *Virginia Brissac* |
| Miss Symonds | *Paula Stone* |
| Herman O'Reilly | *Bobby Gordon* |
| Tommy | *Frank Orth* |
| Dr. Maguire | *Howard Hickman* |
| Sound Mixer | *Ferdinand Schumann-Heink* |

Sherry Scott is the operations manager of a national radio chain owned by Mr. Reynolds. In looking around for good spicy radio material to be hammered into a serial play, Reynolds stumbles upon the Glory Penbrook murder case, a crime committed twenty years before by a woman who still lives.

Glory Penbrook, however, is now living a respectable life. Her daughter, Edith, is about to marry. Thus, with the publicity about the forthcoming marriage in all the newspapers, Reynolds believes he will have a great "audience-builder."

Sherry Scott is very much opposed to the program, especially when he learns that Glory is still alive. But since he is only an employee he must do as he is told. Sherry is a hard-drinking, two-fisted young man.

When the former Glory Penbrook (she is now Mrs. Martha Carstairs) hears that the story of her crime is to be dragged out again and broadcast to the world, she is frantic. She knows that it will ruin her daughter's happiness. She and her husband do everything in their power to stop the malicious broadcast. But Reynolds will not even listen to them. Scott, too, begs Reynolds to forget the program, but Reynolds already has been offered $125,000 for the play and will not cancel it.

Meanwhile, William Sims's parents (he is Edith's fiancé) go to Mr. and Mrs. Carstairs and demand that they break their daughter's engagement. They will not have their son marrying the daughter of a murderess, the Simses say. Edith and William know nothing of all this. They are going on with their plans for the big wedding.

When all hope fades, both Mrs. Carstairs and her husband take their own lives. Edith and William find them dead. They learn about the radio program and that Martha Carstairs was really Glory Penbrook.

Edith goes to the radio station to kill Reynolds. She is followed by William, who arrives in time to hit her arm as she shoots and send the bullet astray. In the face of his parents' wrath, William reavows his love for Edith.

Sherry Scott resigns. But before he does, he fires his pretty secretary, Alma, after which he asks if she will take a job as his wife. She says yes.

With
Barton
MacLane
and
Edward G.
Robinson

With Joan Blondell

# Bullets Or Ballots

Johnny Blake, former detective and head of New York's famed strong-arm squad, has been relegated to a patrolman's beat. He is finally thrown out of the police force for slugging Police Commissioner McLaren.

This convinces Kruger that McLaren and Blake are washed up and that Blake is through with the police department. Kruger needs a man like Blake to show him how to defeat the law. Thus, Kruger hires Blake.

Bugs Fenner has always hated Blake. He will not accept the former detective as an ally. His trigger finger is itching to write the *finis* over Blake's body. But he is afraid of Kruger, who is the only one who knows the identities of the higher-ups, and Fenner knows what would happen to him without protection.

Blake is jailed for slugging another policeman, and in jail he meets McLaren. The audience discovers that Blake is actually working with the police, trying to learn who the real bosses of the syndicate are. Only Kruger knows.

Fenner is thrown out of the gang by Kruger for killing a man, and Fenner, in a rage, kills Kruger. Blake has taken over the numbers game for the syndicate, and Lee Morgan, his former girl friend, grows to hate him.

With Kruger gone, the bosses send for Blake, who has made good in a big way, and make him head of the gang.

Having found out who the bosses are, Blake orders their offices raided when he goes to deliver the weekly receipts.

But Fenner discovers that Blake is working with the police. Lee Morgan unwittingly tells him where Blake is, and Fenner goes to shoot it out. Fenner is killed in the exchange of shots and Blake is severely wounded.

Meanwhile, Lee learns that she has sent Blake to his doom and races to warn him. She is too late. She learns that he is not a traitor to the police department, and is anxious to have him forgive her. She finds him walking along the sidewalk. Without knowing that he is wounded, she drives him to the offices of the supreme council of the rackets.

Blake enters through a series of strong doors, which are opened only for him. The police rush the office and arrest the board of directors as a whole. They use the money Blake has brought as evidence.

Blake dies in McLaren's arms.

Directed by William Keighley. Screenplay by Seton I. Miller. From a story by Martin Mooney and Seton I. Miller. Release date, June 1936. A Warner Brothers-First National Picture.

| | |
|---|---|
| Johnny Blake | *Edward G. Robinson* |
| Lee Morgan | *Joan Blondell* |
| Al Kruger | *Barton MacLane* |
| Bugs Fenner | *Humphrey Bogart* |
| Herman | *Frank McHugh* |
| Captain Dan McLaren | *Joseph King* |
| Driscoll | *Richard Purcell* |
| Wires | *George E. Stone* |
| Grand Jury Spokesman | *Joseph Crehan* |
| Bryant | *Henry O'Neill* |
| Hollister | *Henry Kolker* |
| Thorndyke | *Gilbert Emery* |
| Caldwell | *Herbert Rawlinson* |
| Nellie | *Louise Beavers* |
| Vinci | *Norman Willis* |
| Crail | *William Pawley* |
| Kelly | *Ralph Remley* |
| Gatley | *Frank Faylen* |

# China Clipper

Directed by Ray Enright. Screenplay by Frank Wead. Release date, August 1936. A Warner Brothers-First National Picture.

| | |
|---|---|
| Dave Logan | Pat O'Brien |
| Jean Logan | Beverly Roberts |
| Tom Collins | Ross Alexander |
| Hap Stuart | Humphrey Bogart |
| Sunny Avery | Marie Wilson |
| Jim Horn | Joseph Crehan |
| Mr. Pierson | Joseph King |
| B. C. Hill | Addison Richards |
| Mother Brunn | Ruth Robinson |
| Dad Brunn | Henry B. Walthall |
| Radio Operator on Clipper | Carlyle Moore, Jr. |
| Copilot on Clipper | Lyle Moraine |
| Copilot on Clipper | Dennis Moore |
| Navigator | Wayne Morris |
| Bill Andrews | Alexander Cross |
| Pilot | William Wright |
| Inspector | Kenneth Harlan |
| Secretary | Anne Nagel |
| Secretary | Marjorie Weaver |
| Radio Operator | Milburn Stone |
| Radio Operator | Owen King |

Dave Logan, former wartime ace, and his wife, Jean, witness the triumphant return of Lindbergh from his transatlantic flight. Sensing that the Lindbergh flight will mark the beginning of new interest in aviation, Dave quits his job and begins to make plans for forming a transpacific airline.

Dave goes to Philadelphia and opens a small airline between that city and Washington. His partners are Tom Collins, a war buddy, and Dad Brunn, an airplane designer. But their backer closes the airline for lack of business. Discouraged, they meet that night at dinner. They decide that Dad should design a plane able to fly across the Pacific. In the meantime they plan test flights from Miami to Havana.

In Miami they are ready for the inaugural flight. Hap Stuart, another wartime ace and a friend of Dave's, has become a member of the group. The flight is made and the line is a success. Dave, with headquarters in New York, continues his plans for a Pacific flight. But Jean has left him and has taken a stenographer's job. Dave, with all the work ahead of him, neglected her.

Dave becomes a hard and stern worker. He has a fight with Hap and fires him.

There follows a period of relentless work, with Dave driving Dad Brunn night and day in an effort to finish his "Clipper" ship. Dave forgets all else in his enthusiasm. When the ship is finished, Dave has a hard time finding anyone to put up the money for the initial trip. He gets the money by promising to give up his holdings in a South American aircraft line if the flight is not completed by a certain date.

The deadline day arrives, and, despite bad weather conditions, Dave orders the "China Clipper" to take off. The first pilot is Hap Stuart. Hap takes off against his better judgment and makes the flight after many hazardous experiences.

When the news is flashed back that the "Clipper" has landed in China, Dad Brunn dies of a heart attack. He has lived to see the victory.

Dave and Jean decide to take a second honeymoon on the famous "China Clipper."

*With Paul Graetz*

*With Margaret Lindsay*

# Isle Of Fury

Val Stevens, a fugitive from justice on a small island in the South Pacific, marries Lucille Gordon. Almost immediately after the wedding, Val is called upon to help rescue Eric Blake and Captain Deever, whose boat is sinking off a reef.

Val is oblivious to the fact that Eric and Deever might represent the law, which is the immediate suspicion of Dr. Hardy, an alcoholic physician. So Val takes Eric to his home, and even goes so far as to trust Lucille to take care of the handsome young man.

Thoroughly convinced that Eric represents the law and sure that he means to take Val away, Hardy chides Eric into accompanying Val on a dangerous trip to a nearby island where the native pearl divers are refusing to work. Then, to the embarrassment of both Eric and Lucille, Val insists his bride accompany them.

Otar, the half-caste foreman of the divers, informs his boss, Val, that the men won't go into the water, because the last two who did never came up. Then, to win the respect of his men, Val dons a diver's outfit and orders that he be lowered into the threatening water. He falls into the clutches of an octopus.

Otar, the conspirator, lets the pump fall overboard, leaving Val to almost certain death, but Eric swims down and saves him. He drags Val to the surface.

While Val, Eric, and Hardy are in the office checking over the books, Captain Deever enters. Gun in hand, he says he's going to turn Val over to the police and collect the reward. Eric knocks the revolver out of Deever's hand, and Deever is mortally wounded. Before taking his last breath, he tells Val that Eric has been making love to Lucille.

Hardy saves the day by describing the beautiful relationship between the couple and telling Val he, Dr. Hardy, has convinced Eric, a policeman, that Val is innocent.

Eric tells Val he will report to his office that he found his man and killed him in self-defense. He then leaves the island.

Directed by Frank McDonald. Screenplay by Robert Andrews and William Jacobs. Based on a novel by Somerset Maugham. Release date, October 1936. A Warner Brothers Picture.

| | |
|---|---|
| Val Stevens | *Humphrey Bogart* |
| Lucille Gordon | *Margaret Lindsay* |
| Eric Blake | *Donald Woods* |
| Captain Deever | *Paul Graetz* |
| Andersen | *Gordon Hart* |
| Dr. Hardy | *E. E. Clive* |
| Otar | *George Regas* |
| Sam | *Sidney Bracy* |
| Kim Lee | *Tetsu Komai* |
| Oh Kay | *Miki Morita* |
| The Rector | *Houseley Stevenson, Sr.* |
| Old Native | *Frank Lackteen* |

# The Great O'Malley

Directed by William Dieterle. Associate Producer, Harry Joe Brown. Executive Producer, Hal B. Wallis. Screenplay by Milton Krims and Tom Reed. Based on a story by Gerald Beaumont. Release date, February 1937. A Warner Brothers Picture.

| | |
|---|---|
| James Aloysius O'Malley | *Pat O'Brien* |
| John Phillips | *Humphrey Bogart* |
| Mrs. Phillips | *Frieda Inescort* |
| Attorney for the Defense | *Henry O'Neill* |
| Pinky Holden | *Hobart Cavanaugh* |
| Mrs. O'Malley | *Mary Gordon* |
| Father Patrick | *Frank Sheridan* |
| Tubby | *Delmar Watson* |
| Barbara Phillips | *Sybil Jason* |
| Judy Nolan | *Ann Sheridan* |
| Captain Cromwell | *Donald Crisp* |
| Motorist | *Craig Reynolds* |
| Doctor | *Gordon Hart* |
| Mrs. Flaherty | *Mabel Colcord* |
| Miss Taylor | *Lillian Harmer* |
| Dr. Larson | *Frank Reicher* |

Officer James O'Malley is a cop who lives by his book of rules. He has no heart. Pinky Holden, a fresh young reporter, ridicules O'Malley in his paper. This infuriates Captain Cromwell, commander of the precinct. Unable to break O'Malley of his habit of handing out tickets for trifling offenses, the captain assigns him to guard a street-crossing in front of a public school.

John Phillips is an unemployed workman. He comes along in his rattletrap car. Its muffler is broken and the exhaust is noisy. That's against the rules in O'Malley's book. He gives Phillips a ticket, which delays him so that he loses his chance at a job he was seeking. He is bitter and resentful.

Phillips goes home sadly to his wife and their little daughter, who has been lame since birth. He gets his war medals and takes them out to pawn. In a squabble with the pawnbroker, he knocks the man out, then, suddenly tempted, he grabs all the money in the till and flees.

O'Malley arrests Phillips—not because of the robbery, but for not fixing the muffler. This brings another blast of ridicule from the newspapers.

O'Malley's only friend is his mother, and even she isn't too sympathetic with his methods.

Little lame Barbara Phillips is knocked down at O'Malley's crossing. He and the child's teacher, Judy Nolan, carry her home. Then he realizes that the little girl is the daughter of the man he has arrested. This knowledge strikes home, and he comes to love the little girl—and the teacher.

O'Malley goes to a great specialist, who performs an operation that restores Barbara to health. He goes before the parole board and wins Phillips' release. He even gets Phillips a job, the one that he caused Phillips to lose in the first place.

Phillips knows none of this, and when he gets out of prison he gets a gun. The two meet on the stairway of Phillips' home. Phillips, half-crazed by his prison term and his fear of persecution, shoots O'Malley. But O'Malley is a changed man. He insists that the shot was an accident.

When he recovers from his wound, O'Malley goes back to duty a different man. He forgets his silly notions about the trivialities of the rule book. He and Phillips become fast friends. Above all, he wins the love of Judy Nolan.

Frank Taylor works in an automobile factory with his friend Ed Jackson. Expecting promotion to foreman, he is bitterly disappointed when Dombrowski, a hard-working foreigner, gets the job.

Frank joins the Black Legion, which fights against the invasion of American rights by foreigners. Instead of being a patriotic organization, the Black Legion is really a racket from which its promoters make thousands. Frank's first assignment as a member of the Legion is to help burn Dombrowski's home and drive him out of town.

This and other activities of the Legion keep the heretofore steady Frank away from home night after night. His nerves shattered, he starts to drink. His devoted wife, Ruth, begins to question him. He becomes sullen and abusive. Finally, he strikes her, and she leaves with their little son to visit her father.

In a drunken moment, he tells Ed of his connection with the Legion and the burning of Dombrowski's home. Now that Ed knows, something must be done.

That night the Legion takes Ed out to horsewhip him into a promise of silence. Ed defies them and knocks down several of his captors. He is just escaping when the Legion chief orders his men to shoot. Frank pulls his gun and fires. To his horror, he kills his best friend.

Anguished and hysterical, Frank flees, but is later captured.

A Black Legion lawyer comes to his cell with a threat to harm Frank's wife and son unless he puts himself entirely in their hands.

When his case comes to trial, the Legion produces Pearl Danvers as a defense witness. She testifies that Frank loved her and that Ed was jealous; that Ed attacked Frank and Frank killed him in self-defense.

When it appears that this testimony will clear him, Frank's conscience asserts itself. He asks to be put on the stand, and in a dramatic recital confesses everything and points out the members of the Black Legion who are in the courtroom. Amid scenes of great excitement, they are all arrested.

In a magnificent charge in which he outlines the true meaning of Americanism and excoriates the false patriots who prey on national and racial prejudices, the judge sentences Frank to life imprisonment.

Directed by Archie L. Mayo. Screenplay by Abem Finkel and William Wister Haines. Based on a story by Robert Lord. Release date, January 1937. A Warner Brothers Picture.

| | |
|---|---|
| Frank Taylor | *Humphrey Bogart* |
| Ed Jackson | *Dick Foran* |
| Ruth Taylor | *Erin O'Brien-Moore* |
| Betty Grogan | *Ann Sheridan* |
| Brown | *Robert Barrat* |
| Pearl Danvers | *Helen Flint* |
| Cliff More | *Joseph Sawyer* |
| Prosecuting Attorney | *Addison Richards* |
| Metcalf | *Eddie Acuff* |
| Mike Grogan | *Clifford Soubier* |
| Billings | *Paul Harvey* |
| Judge | *Samuel Hinds* |
| Tommy Smith | *John Litel* |
| Osgood | *Charles Halton* |
| Charlie | *Francis Sayles* |
| Jones | *Harry Hayden* |
| Alf Hargrave | *Alonzo Price* |
| Buddy Taylor | *Dickie Jones* |
| Mrs. Grogan | *Dorothy Vaughan* |
| Joe Dombrowski | *Henry Brandon* |
| Nick Strumpas | *Pat C. Flick* |
| Barham | *Paul Stanton* |
| Old Man Dombrowski | *Egon Brecher* |

*With Erin O'Brien-Moore (above)*

# San Quentin

Directed by Lloyd Bacon. Associate Producer, Sam Bischoff. Executive Producer, Hal B. Wallis. Screenplay by Peter Milne and Humphrey Cobb. Story by Robert Tasker and John Bright. Release date, August 1937. A Warner Brothers-First National Picture.

| | |
|---|---|
| Capt. Stephen Jameson | *Pat O'Brien* |
| Joe "Red" Kennedy | *Humphrey Bogart* |
| May | *Ann Sheridan* |
| Lt. Druggin | *Barton MacLane* |
| "Sailor Boy" Hansen | *Joseph Sawyer* |
| Helen | *Veda Ann Borg* |
| Mickey Callahan | *James Robbins* |
| Warden Taylor | *Joseph King* |
| Captain | *Gordon Oliver* |
| Dopey | *Garry Owen* |
| Venetti | *Marc Lawrence* |
| Lieutenant | *Emmett Vogan* |
| Convict | *William Pawley* |
| Convict | *Al Hill* |
| Prison Runner | *Max Wagner* |
| Convict | *George Lloyd* |
| Fink | *Ernie Adams* |

Captain Stephen Jameson is ordered to San Quentin prison as captain of the yard to replace the acting captain, Druggin, a prison official of the old school. There has been considerable trouble in the penitentiary, and the warden believes that an army man can discipline the convicts.

On the night before he starts his new job, Jameson goes to a night club and falls in love with the blues singer, May Kennedy. Her brother, Red, has just been sentenced to San Quentin for robbery. Because she is bitter about prisons, Jameson doesn't tell her he is the new captain of the yard.

From the first, Red has trouble. He gets into a fight and is placed in solitary. When he gets out of solitary, May comes to see him, and he asks for money. A guard sees her give it to him, and May is taken to Jameson's office. On learning who he is, she refuses to see him again. However, after Jameson takes an interest in Red, persuades him to behave himself, and begins making life easier for him, she relents and promises to marry him.

Red begins to admire the yard captain, and when Jameson heroically risks his life to save a group of convicts from a crazy prisoner with a machine gun, Red is completely sold on the new official and decides to rebuild his life.

Meanwhile, Druggin, angered because Jameson has been made yard captain over him, starts plotting. Learning that some prisoners are going to attempt to escape from the road gang on which Red has been placed, Druggin tells Red that Jameson has designs on his sister. Red determines to escape and kill Jameson. With another prisoner he makes a break from the road gang. The other convict is killed, but Red gets away and goes to May's apartment. There he finds Jameson and is going to shoot him, but May tells her brother she loves Jameson. Deeply ashamed, Red promises to go back to prison of his own accord. As he leaves the apartment, he is shot, but gets away from the police. He staggers up to the gates of San Quentin and dies after giving himself up.

*With
Pat
O'Brien*

*With
Ann
Sheridan
and
Pat
O'Brien*

*With Bette Davis, Mayo Methot, and Rosalind Marquis*

# Marked Woman

Johnny Vanning, who has been organizing and taking over nearly everything in the city, arrives at last to look over the night club "Intime" and its hostesses. These are Mary, Florrie, Gabby, Emmy Lou, and Estelle. In a speech full of quiet menace, Vanning explains that he is taking over the place, changing it into a clip joint where suckers will come for a heavy trimming, and where the hostesses will make fifty times more than ever before. But they must kick back some of their earnings to him, to square police trouble, to use for bail bonds, and so on.

Among the changes he orders in the club are a refinishing in garish modern style, and the firing of Estelle, because she is too old! Mary intercedes in Estelle's behalf, and in a spirited exchange with Vanning incurs his dislike, arouses his interest in her personally, and convinces him she will be, as she promises, a valuable asset to his business. So he lets Estelle stay.

When the clip joint is operating, Mary is innocently involved in a murder investigation which causes all the girls to be arrested. With them also is Mary's young sister, Betty, from whom Mary has been trying to keep the knowledge that she is a hostess in a night club. David Graham, an assistant district attorney, zealously undertakes to prosecute Vanning, but is double-crossed by the defense lawyer with the assistance of Mary. As Graham had trusted Mary, he is bitterly disillusioned; so is Mary's sister, Betty.

Mary turns against Vanning at the risk of her own life when Betty, lured into one of the boss's parties, flees from an amorous guest and is killed. Emmy Lou, who is present, is the key to this murder, so she is kidnapped, and Mary is brutally beaten and marked on the face with a knife slash because she went to Graham to testify and seek his help. The other girls, afraid for their lives, refuse to be of any help to the law.

Vanning, worried by Graham's determined attempts to connect him with the murder, arranges to have Emmy Lou rubbed out. She escapes and, with Mary, tells her story to Graham. So do the other girls, and Vanning is brought to trial with his henchmen and convicted on four counts.

Directed by Lloyd Bacon. Associate Producer, Lou Edelman. Executive Producer, Hal B. Wallis. Screenplay by Robert Rossen and Abem Finkel. Release date, April 1937. A Warner Brothers-First National Picture.

| | |
|---|---|
| Mary | Bette Davis |
| David Graham | Humphrey Bogart |
| Gabby | Lola Lane |
| Emmy Lou | Isabel Jewell |
| Johnny Vanning | Eduardo Ciannelli |
| Betty | Jane Bryan |
| Florrie | Rosalind Marquis |
| Estelle | Mayo Methot |
| Louie | Allen Jenkins |
| Gordon | John Litel |
| Charlie | Ben Welden |
| Ralph Krawford | Damian O'Flynn |
| Sheldon | Henry O'Neill |
| Lawyer at Jail | Raymond Hatton |
| Head Waiter | Carlos San Martin |
| Crandall | William B. Davidson |
| Eddie | Kenneth Harlan |
| George Beler | Robert Strange |
| Bell Captain | James Robbins |
| Mr. Truble | Arthur Aylesworth |
| Vincent | John Sheehan |
| Mac | Sam Wren |
| Ferguson | Edwin Stanley |
| Henchman | Allen Matthews |
| Henchman | Alan Davis |
| Detective | Guy Usher |

# Kid Galahad

Directed by Michael Curtiz. Screenplay
by Seton I. Miller. From the *Saturday Evening
Post* story by Francis Wallace. Release date,
May 1937. A Warner Brothers Picture.

| | |
|---|---|
| Nick Donati | *Edward G. Robinson* |
| Fluff | *Bette Davis* |
| Turkey Morgan | *Humphrey Bogart* |
| Ward Guisenberry (Kid Galahad) | *Wayne Morris* |
| Marie | *Jane Bryan* |
| Silver Jackson | *Harry Carey* |
| Chuck McGraw | *William Haade* |
| Mrs. Donati | *Soledad Jiminez* |
| Joe Taylor | *Joe Cunningham* |
| Buzz Barrett | *Ben Welden* |
| Brady | *Joseph Crehan* |
| The Redhead | *Veda Ann Borg* |
| Barney | *Frank Faylen* |
| Gunman | *Harland Tucker* |
| Sam | *Bob Evans* |
| Burke | *Hank Hankinson* |
| O'Brien | *Bob Nestell* |
| Denbaugh | *Jack Kranz* |
| Referee | *George Blake* |

Nick Donati, an honest fight manager, has just lost his fighter and most of his money in a fight that was fixed by sinister Turkey Morgan. Nick and his girl, Fluff, throw a big party to spend all the rest of their money. Turkey and heavyweight contender Chuck McGraw crash the party. McGraw insults Fluff, and the bellhop, Ward Guisenberry, defending her honor, floors McGraw.

Nick thinks he has found a new contender, and when McGraw demands revenge, Nick agrees to have Ward fight McGraw's brother, even though Ward will be unmercifully beaten.

But Ward wins by a knockout. Then Ward knocks out Turkey Morgan. Ward is forced to go into hiding, and he falls in love with Marie Donati, Nick's sister. Nick doesn't like it at all. He has always wanted to keep her away from the dirty fight racket. He hustles Ward away from the hide-out and takes him on the road, where he knocks out almost everyone that he fights.

Fluff dubs Ward "Kid Galahad." Then she quarrels with Nick and leaves him. Marie comes to New York to see Ward even though Nick has warned her not to. Nick grows to hate "Kid Galahad," and to get even, he sets up a fight with McGraw, who has become champion. He is sure that Kid Galahad will be beaten, and he sells out his own fighter to Turkey by promising to have Ward come out slugging against McGraw.

Since Nick bets all his money against his own fighter, Turkey thinks that he is on the level, but he warns Nick that at the first sign of a double-cross he'll be rubbed out.

When the big fight begins, Ward is knocked down again and again, battered half-unconscious.

Suddenly Ward's chance comes. He blasts McGraw down and out.

The police hustle the new champ and his manager to their dressing rooms. But Turkey has outwitted them; pistol in hand, he confronts Nick, Ward, and a trainer in the shower room. Nick tries to down him with a shot through his coat pocket just as Turkey's gun begins to blaze. Turkey falls dead. Nick sags to the floor, mortally wounded.

Dying, the fight manager gives his blessing to Ward and Marie, and with his final breath, brags to Fluff that he has finally built a champion.

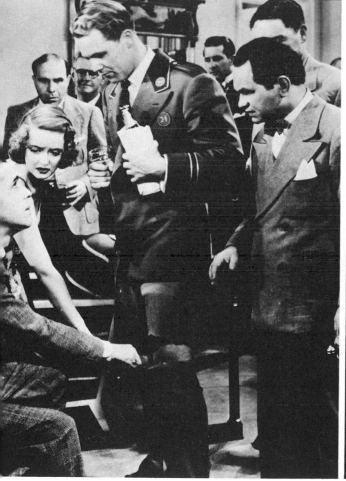

*With Bette Davis, Wayne Morris, and Edward G. Robinson*

*With Wayne Morris, Edward G. Robinson, and William Haade*

*With Joel McCrea and Allen Jenkins*

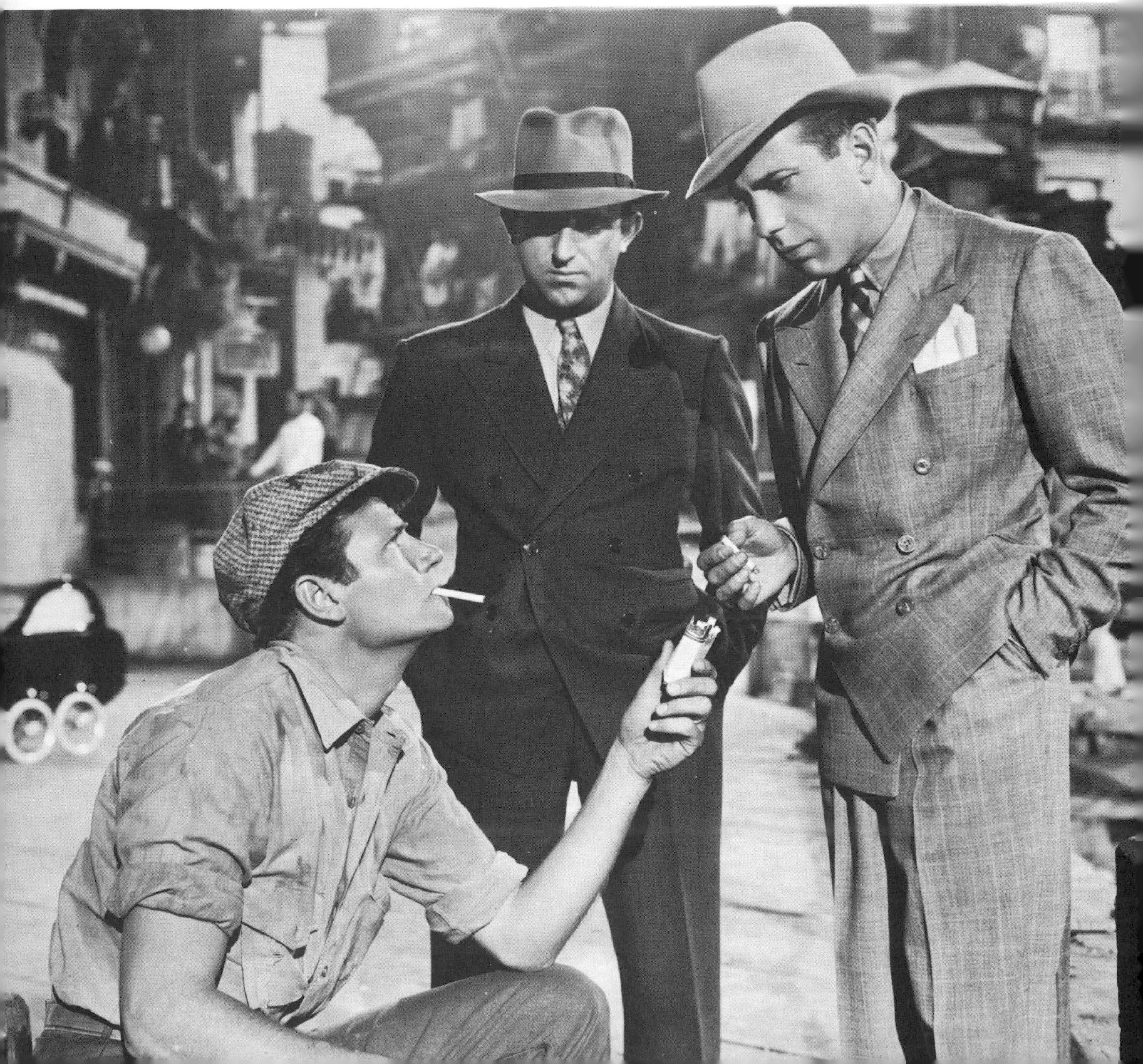

# Dead End

Swarming near the slimy piers of the backwash of the East River is a group of slum hoodlums who pass their time in gambling and petty thievery.

Their idols are the gangsters and public enemies, many of whom, including notorious Baby Face Martin, have risen from their own ranks.

The leader, Tommy, has been reared by his sister, Drina, who has struggled to save both from their degrading surroundings. She loves Dave, an out-of-work architect who desperately wants to escape from the neighborhood. He is infatuated with Kay, who is being kept by a businessman in a luxurious apartment.

The kids pounce on Philip, a young boy, and steal his watch.

Baby Face Martin, sinister gangster, returns. His face has been changed by plastic surgery. He comes home to see his mother and his old girl friend, Francey. His mother throws him out of the house, and he is shocked that Francey has taken to the easy life.

Dave recognizes Martin, who warns him to keep quiet.

Martin teaches the young hoodlums to use a knife, and *he* uses it on Philip's father when he comes to get the watch back.

Martin plans to kidnap Philip, but Dave interferes. Martin stabs him. The wound is only superficial. Dave kills Martin.

The police come and tell Dave that he will get a reward for killing Martin.

Spit squeals on Tommy. Tommy evades the police and goes into hiding. Drina and Dave convince Tommy to give himself up to the police. They tell him that if he does, they will go easy on him.

Despite Drina's plea that reform school will ruin Tommy, the police will not release him. Drina finds solace in Dave's arms, hopeful that the reward Dave will get for killing Martin will enable him to hire a lawyer who will save Tommy from the dread reform school and enable them to leave this dead end forever.

Directed by William Wyler. Adapted by Lillian Hellman from the Norman Bel Geddes production of the Sidney Kingsley drama. Release date, August 1937. A Samuel Goldwyn Production, released by United Artists.

| | |
|---|---|
| Drina | *Sylvia Sidney* |
| Dave | *Joel McCrea* |
| Baby Face Martin | *Humphrey Bogart* |
| Kay | *Wendy Barrie* |
| Francey | *Claire Trevor* |
| Hunk | *Allen Jenkins* |
| Mrs. Martin | *Marjorie Main* |
| Tommy | *Billy Halop* |
| Dippy | *Huntz Hall* |
| Angel | *Bobby Jordan* |
| Spit | *Leo Gorcey* |
| T.B. | *Gabriel Dell* |
| Milty | *Bernard Punsley* |
| Philip | *Charles Peck* |
| Mr. Griswold | *Minor Watson* |
| Mulligan | *James Burke* |
| Doorman | *Ward Bond* |
| Mrs. Connell | *Elizabeth Risdon* |
| Mrs. Fenner | *Esther Dale* |
| Mr. Pascagli | *George Humbert* |
| Governess | *Marcelle Corday* |

# Stand-In

Directed by Tay Garnett. Produced by
Walter Wanger. Screenplay by Gene Towne
and Graham Baker. Based on the story by
Clarence Kelland. Release date,
October 1937. A United Artists Picture.

| | |
|---|---|
| Atterbury Dodd | *Leslie Howard* |
| Lester Plum | *Joan Blondell* |
| Quintain | *Humphrey Bogart* |
| Koslofski | *Alan Mowbray* |
| Cheri | *Marla Shelton* |
| Nassau | *C. Henry Gordon* |
| Potts | *Jack Carson* |
| Pettypacker Jr. | *J. C. Nugent* |
| Pettypacker Sr. | *Tully Marshall* |
| Pettypacker | *William V. Mong* |

Atterbury Dodd, brilliant young executive, is sent to Hollywood
to oversee his bank's investment in the Colossal Film Company.
There is a plot afoot in Hollywood, involving Ivor Nassau,
Koslofski, a director, and Thelma Cheri, an exotic star, to waste
so much money that Dodd will recommend that his bank sell
Colossal to them at a very low figure. The plotters know that
there is only one man standing in their way, Douglas Quintain,
Colossal's operating chief, clever when he is sober, but something else again when drunk. But there is little Quintain can do
about the waste of money because Koslofski and Cheri have
strong contracts.

Once in Hollywood, Dodd "accidentally" meets a beautiful
young woman with the unusual name of Lester Plum. He visits
the set where Koslofski and Cheri are making their "epic." They
are wasting money right and left, but there is nothing Quintain
can do.

Dodd hires Lester as his secretary. He doesn't know that she
is Cheri's stand-in. When Quintain previews the "epic" he sees
that it is terrible. To put Colossal further in debt, Koslofski suggests retakes which will cost a fortune. Dodd decides to tell his
bank to sell the studio. Lester protests. She says that thousands
of people will lose their jobs. Dodd asks Quintain to help save
the studio.

Quintain agrees to recut the picture, provided that there is
no interference from Koslofski. Nassau appeals to the bank
directly, over Dodd's head, and the studio is ordered sold.

But Dodd, spurred on by Lester, defies Nassau to take possession of the plant. Quintain works feverishly to re-edit the
picture, and when he completes the job, a gorilla is the hero,
Cheri plays a minor role, and the "epic" has become an up-
roarious comedy and a sure box-office hit.

Dodd ousts Nassau by threatening to charge him with conspiracy. Colossal is saved for the stockholders and employees.
Most important of all, Lester makes Dodd realize he has cor-
puscles instead of figures in his blood, especially when she is in
his arms.

*With Nat
Pendleton
and
Louise
Fazenda*

*With Frank
McHugh
and Nat
Pendleton*

# Swing Your Lady

Ed Hatch, wrestling promoter; Joe Skopapoulous, "The Wrestling Hercules"; Popeye Bronson, the trainer; and Shiner Ward, Hatch's assistant, arrive in a small town in Missouri absolutely broke. Their tour has been a failure.

One day Hatch gets stuck in the mud, and an Amazon of a blacksmith easily lifts the car out of the muck. She is Sadie Horn. An idea occurs to Hatch—he will match Sadie to wrestle Joe.

Joe accidentally meets Sadie, and they are immediately attracted to each other. Hatch and the others finally break it to Joe that he is to wrestle a woman. They do not know that Sadie has already tipped him off. But Joe won't go through with the fight, since he is in love with Sadie. Sadie is angry, for she wanted to buy a bedroom set with the $100 she was to get for the match.

In the meantime, Noah Wulliver, Sadie's boy friend, comes to drive Joe away with his squirrel gun. As Sadie forces Noah to stop shooting, Hatch gets another idea. It will be a grudge match between Noah and Joe, with Sadie going to the winner, and Sadie receiving the money.

On the night of the sport club's dance, Hatch discovers that Sadie is madly in love with Joe and plans to marry him, regardless of who wins the match. Desperately, Hatch lies, telling Sadie that Joe is married and has a family. Sadie tells Joe what she thinks of him, picks him off his feet, and slams him to the ground.

The match is a sellout, but Joe's heart isn't in his work. Sadie has turned him down, and Hatch has ordered him to lose.

A wire is received offering the winner of the fight a match at Madison Square Garden. Hatch tries to signal Joe that he now wants him to win, but the heartsick grappler fails to understand. Sadie frenziedly yells for Noah to throw Joe, and Joe decides that he has had enough. He can't throw the match. In a matter of seconds he has Noah pinned and is the winner.

The crowd demands that Joe, as the winner, get Sadie, but she announces Joe is married. Joe forces Hatch to confess his lie.

He does, and they all start off for New York in Hatch's car.

Directed by Ray Enright. Executive Producer, Hall B. Wallis. Associate Producer, Sam Bischoff. Screenplay by Joseph Schrank and Maurice Leo. Adapted from the play by Charles Robinson and Kenyon Nicholson. Release date, January 1938. A Warner Brothers Picture.

| | |
|---|---|
| Ed Hatch | *Humphrey Bogart* |
| Popeye | *Frank McHugh* |
| Sadie | *Louise Fazenda* |
| Joe | *Nat Pendleton* |
| Cookie | *Penny Singleton* |
| Shiner | *Allen Jenkins* |
| Waldo | *Leon Weaver* |
| Ollie Davis | *Frank Weaver* |
| Mrs. Davis | *Elviry Weaver* |
| Jack Miller | *Ronald Reagan* |
| Noah | *Daniel Boone Savage* |
| Smith | *Hugh O'Connell* |
| Rufe | *Tommy Bupp* |
| Len | *Sonny Bupp* |
| Mattie | *Joan Howard* |
| Mabel | *Sue Moore* |
| Hotel Proprietor | *Olin Howlin* |
| Specialty Dancer | *Sammy White* |

# Men Are Such Fools

Directed by Busby Berkeley. Screenplay by Norman Reilly Raine and Horace Jackson. From a *Saturday Evening Post* story by Faith Baldwin. Release date, July 1938. A Warner Brothers Picture.

| | |
|---|---|
| Jimmy Hall | *Wayne Morris* |
| Linda Lawrence | *Priscilla Lane* |
| Harry Galleon | *Humphrey Bogart* |
| Nancy | *Penny Singleton* |
| Harvey Bates | *Hugh Herbert* |
| Wanda Townsend | *Marcia Ralston* |
| Bill Dalton | *Gene Lockhart* |
| Mrs. Dalton | *Kathleen Lockhart* |
| Tad | *Johnnie Davis* |
| George Onslow | *Donald Briggs* |
| Beatrice Harris | *Mona Barrie* |
| Mrs. Pinkel | *Reine Riano* |
| Rudolf | *Claude Allister* |
| Bill Collyer | *James Nolan* |
| Mrs. Nelson | *Nedda Harrigan* |

Linda Lawrence is the charming secretary of Harvey Bates, an account executive of a big New York advertising agency. Linda lives with her girl friend, Nancy, who is very much in love and about to be married to Tad. Nancy tries to sell Linda on the idea that matrimony is to be preferred to success in the advertising world, especially since Jimmy Hall is crazy about her and wants to marry her.

However, Linda is ambitious. She is convinced that Jimmy will never come any closer to success than a house in the Bronx. As the first rung in the ladder of success, she conceives the idea of selling canned orange juice to the public as "Fruit-Tea Cocktail," good for hangovers. It saves one of the agency's largest accounts.

Using her natural charm, Linda impresses Harvey Bates, and Bates in turn introduces her to Onslow and to Beatrice Harris, smart businesswoman of the agency.

Jimmy is at first awed and then indignant at the rapidity with which Linda is getting ahead in the business world. He begs her to drop everything and marry him.

Beatrice invites them to her country home. Jimmy finally persuades Linda to become engaged to him. But Linda meets Harry Galleon, the big man of the agency. Galleon has been having an affair with Beatrice and is more or less engaged to Wanda Townsend.

Linda decides that, although she is engaged to Jimmy, she can use her influence with Galleon to get ahead in the business world.

Three months pass, and Galleon is trying to win Linda. Subtly he flatters her ego and helps her to get ahead while shoving Jimmy into the background. After a row with Jimmy, Linda finally agrees to quit her job.

She tries to stir Jimmy's initiative, but he refuses all help. Linda leaves him and returns to the agency.

However, when Jimmy discovers over the radio that Linda is about to go to Paris with Galleon, he goes to the studio and beats Galleon up. He arrives at the boat too late to catch Linda, but discovers that she has not sailed. She has planted the speech on the radio to test Jimmy's love.

Meanwhile, Galleon is aboard and expects to find Linda in his cabin. Instead, he finds Wanda, who has been told to meet him there by a telegram from Linda.

*With Priscilla Lane*

*With
Harry
Cording
and
Cy Kendall*

# Crime School

Mark Braden, director of a settlement house in New York, is in court when six young hoodlums are tried on charges of petty thievery and assault on a junkman.

He becomes interested in Sue Warren, sister of one of the boys. But his well-intentioned advances are misinterpreted and repulsed.

The boys are sent to Gatesville Reformatory, presided over by Superintendent Morgan, a political grafter, and his henchman and head keeper, Cooper.

There, Frankie Warren, leader of the boys—Squirt, Bugs, Spike, Goofy, and Fats—runs afoul of the administration and is beaten and placed in solitary.

But Mark Braden is appointed Commissioner of Corrections and arrives to find the institution maladministered. He suspends Morgan and most of the guards and institutes the honor system among the boy inmates.

Cooper, who at first has Braden fooled, stays and works against him in secret while keeping in touch with Morgan, who goes to the city to talk it over with the boss.

Meanwhile, Braden gains ground with Sue Warren in New York. But the conspirators, learning of his interest in her, work against Braden in two directions. Through the medium of a petty mobster in her tenement neighborhood, they make Sue believe Braden was behind the earlier mistreatment of her brother. And at the reformatory, Cooper poisons Frankie's mind against Braden by veiled allegations about his relations with his sister.

Just as Braden wins a parole for the six youths, Cooper engineers a jail break which lets the sextet escape and start out to gun Braden. The head keeper then "discovers" the youths have fled, calls the reporters, and places the blame on Braden's "newfangled" methods of reformatory administration.

Quick-witted work on Braden's part, however, enables him not only to foil the plot but to reveal Cooper in his true light. The boys are saved from committing a tragic error, and Braden and Sue are on their way to being united.

Directed by Lewis Seiler. Screenplay by Crane Wilbur and Vincent Sherman. From a story by Crane Wilbur. Release date, May 1938. A Warner Brothers-First National Picture.

| | |
|---|---|
| Mark Braden | *Humphrey Bogart* |
| Sue Warren | *Gale Page* |
| Frankie Warren | *Billy Halop* |
| Squirt | *Bobby Jordan* |
| Goofy | *Huntz Hall* |
| Spike | *Leo Gorcey* |
| Fats | *Bernard Punsley* |
| Bugs | *Gabriel Dell* |
| Red | *George Offerman, Jr.* |
| Cooper | *Weldon Heyburn* |
| Morgan | *Cy Kendall* |
| Judge Clinton | *Charles Trowbridge* |
| Joe Delaney | *Milburn Stone* |
| Guard | *Harry Cording* |
| Old Doctor | *Spencer Charters* |
| New Doctor | *Donald Briggs* |
| Commissioner | *Frank Jaquet* |
| Mrs. Burke | *Helen MacKellar* |
| Mr. Burke | *Al Bridge* |
| Mrs. Hawkins | *Sybil Harris* |
| Nick Papadopolo | *Paul Porcasi* |
| John Brower | *Jack Mower* |
| Junkie | *Frank Otto* |
| Officer Hogan | *Ed Gargan* |
| Schwartz | *James B. Carson* |

# The Amazing Dr. Clitterhouse

Directed by Anatole Litvak. Executive Producer, Hal B. Wallis. Associate Producer, Robert Lord. Screenplay by John Wexley and John Huston. From the play by Barre Lyndon. Release date, July 1938. An Anatole Litvak Production for First National Pictures-Warner Brothers.

| | |
|---|---|
| Dr. Clitterhouse | *Edward G. Robinson* |
| Jo Keller | *Claire Trevor* |
| Rocks Valentine | *Humphrey Bogart* |
| Okay | *Allen Jenkins* |
| Inspector Lane | *Donald Crisp* |
| Nurse Randolph | *Gale Page* |
| Judge | *Henry O'Neill* |
| Prosecuting Attorney | *John Litel* |
| Grant | *Thurston Hall* |
| Butch | *Maxie Rosenbloom* |
| Pal | *Bert Hanlon* |
| Rabbit | *Curt Bois* |
| Tug | *Ward Bond* |
| Popus | *Vladimir Sokoloff* |
| Candy | *Billy Wayne* |
| Lt. Johnson | *Robert Homans* |
| Foreman of Jury | *Irving Bacon* |

Unknown to anyone except his nurse, the famous physician and scientist Dr. Clitterhouse engages in burglaries in order to make a scientific study of criminal reactions to fear and excitement and to study their psychology.

Through his police connections, Clitterhouse learns the names of the best fences and invades the stronghold of the leading one, Jo Keller, who bosses a choice gang of expert jewel thieves. He also meets Rocks Valentine, their chief, and Butch, Jo's bodyguard.

Under Clitterhouse's direction they carry out numerous robberies—and all the while Clitterhouse makes copious notes and checks the reactions of the band, physically and mentally.

Jo is fascinated by the man, whose name none of them know and who is dubbed, "The Professor." Rocks resents Clitterhouse—especially because Jo is falling in love with "The Professor."

Clitterhouse's research is almost completed, but he plans one more great job—the looting of a great fur warehouse. He is determined to leave the gang because he fears that he's beginning to like the life of a criminal. The robbery is a success, and Clitterhouse returns to his respectable life.

Rocks learns his real identity and this gives Rocks a hold on the doctor. He blackmails him into continuing the life of crime.

Clitterhouse pretends to accept the inevitable and proposes a toast—a toast to crime. He fixes the drinks, and Rocks downs his in one gulp and dies.

Later, suspicion points to Jo's mob, and Butch breaks and tells about "The Professor." Inspector Lane is loath to believe Clitterhouse is to blame, but finally makes the arrest after permitting him to consult with his lawyer. The lawyer tells him he is undoubtedly insane and will escape with his life.

At the trial the jury is confused by the highly conflicting testimony of insanity experts and, after a long deadlock, finally decides to ask Clitterhouse several questions. He answers frankly and has apparently convicted himself when the foreman asks if he thinks he was insane when he committed the crime.

When Clitterhouse honestly says he does not, the jury promptly acquits him on the theory that anyone offering insanity as his defense and then insisting that he is sane—must be insane.

*With Claire Trevor, Maxie Rosenbloom, Edward G. Robinson, and Allen Jenkins*

81

The governor appoints Hugh Allison as special prosecutor to end the racketeering activities of Martin, but his work is hampered because people are afraid to testify.

Martin moves to take control of the trucking business by forcing drivers to join a protective association. Denny Jordan and his partner, Horse Wilson, small truck owners, fight the racketeers and encourage others to do the same.

Nora, Denny's wife, is pregnant. She collapses after Denny is beaten, and Martin's men warn her to tell him to stop fighting. Denny learns that it will take a great deal of money to pay Nora's hospital bills. He then robs Martin's office of the money needed to send Nora away. Martin and his men come to Denny's apartment. Martin tells Denny that he won't hurt him if he joins the Association, and to protect Nora, Denny joins. He is ostracized by his friends.

With the truck drivers lined up 100 per cent, Martin starts to organize the commission men, wrecking stores and ruining food-stuffs. A victim of the terrorism is Horse, who has gone into the tomato business. Pop, fighting secretary of the old truckmen's union, is killed when he gives evidence to Allison.

Nora returns with the baby and tells Denny they are through because he joined Martin. At Pop's funeral, truck drivers plot to prevent Denny from getting a last glimpse of his old friend. Denny is picked up and thrown in jail under a new law which makes it an offense to withhold evidence.

Martin calls a general strike of truck drivers which will cut off the city's food supply and force the commission men to line up with him. Allison releases Denny from jail, figuring his manhood will assert itself and that he will induce the strikers to go back to work. Horse, attempting to get the trucks moving, is shot by one of Martin's men just as Denny gets there. Denny inspires the men to break the strike, and then he goes to Martin's apartment.

He is beating up Martin when detectives arrive and arrest the racketeer. Denny gives Allison the evidence necessary to convict Martin, and racketeering is driven from New York. Denny and Nora are reunited, and all the men go back to work.

Directed by Lloyd Bacon. Screenplay by Robert Rossen and Leonardo Bercovici. Release date, August 1938. Produced by Cosmopolitan and released by Warner Brothers.

| | |
|---|---|
| Martin | *Humphrey Bogart* |
| Denny Jordan | *George Brent* |
| Nora Jordan | *Gloria Dickson* |
| Horse Wilson | *Allen Jenkins* |
| Allison | *Walter Abel* |
| Governor | *Henry O'Neill* |
| Gladys | *Penny Singleton* |
| Crane | *Anthony Averill* |
| Pop | *Oscar O'Shea* |
| Charlie Smith | *Elliott Sullivan* |
| Mrs. Smith | *Fay Helm* |
| Joe | *Joe Downing* |
| Gus | *Norman Wallis* |
| Kimball | *Don Rowan* |

*With George Brent*

# Angels With Dirty Faces

Directed by Michael Curtiz. Screenplay by John Wexley and Warren Duff. From a story by Rowland Brown. Release date, November 1938. A Warner Brothers-First National Picture.

| | |
|---|---|
| Rocky Sullivan | *James Cagney* |
| Jerry Connolly | *Pat O'Brien* |
| James Frazier | *Humphrey Bogart* |
| Laury Ferguson | *Ann Sheridan* |
| Mac Keefer | *George Bancroft* |
| Soapy | *Billy Halop* |
| Swing | *Bobby Jordon* |
| Bim | *Leo Gorcey* |
| Pasty | *Gabriel Dell* |
| Crab | *Huntz Hall* |
| Hunky | *Bernard Punsley* |
| Steve | *Joe Downing* |
| Edwards | *Edward Pawley* |
| Blackie | *Adrian Morris* |
| Rocky (as a boy) | *Frankie Burke* |
| Jerry (as a boy) | *William Tracy* |
| Laury (as a child) | *Marilyn Knowlden* |

St. Brendan's Church Choir

Two boys from the slums, Rocky Sullivan and Jerry Connolly, break into a freight car and steal some fountain pens. Attempting to escape, Jerry is successful, but Rocky is caught and sent to reform school.

Years pass, and Rocky is now a big-shot gangster being released from prison, where he has gone to take the rap for his attorney, James Frazier, who has promised him $100,000 upon his release. He returns to his old haunts and finds Jerry, a priest, striving to make good citizens out of slum boys.

Jerry arranges for Rocky's lodging and a meeting with the latter's childhood sweetheart, Laury, hoping that she will mend Rocky's ways.

As Rocky walks through the old neighborhood, he is set upon by six hoodlums who rob him and flee to a hide-out, which turns out to be Rocky's old hideaway. He follows them easily, and when they find out who he is, they idolize him.

Frazier, now tied up with Mac Keefer, a big politician, decides to double-cross Rocky when the latter asks for his money, and sends out thugs to kill him. Rocky, walking with Laury, outwits the gangsters, goes to Frazier's offices, and loots the safe of records that implicate high city officials in racketeering.

Both racketeers are more amenable now, and after a few scrapes with the police, they make Rocky a partner in Keefer's night club. Laury is given the job as hostess. When Jerry learns of this, he decides to clean up the town and, with the aid of a large newspaper, goes to work.

On the eve of the grand jury investigation, Rocky learns that Frazier and Keefer plan to kill him. He shoots both men. The police move in and, after a running gun battle, capture Rocky.

Tried for murder and sentenced to the chair, Rocky becomes the great hero to all the slum boys. Reading he will go to the chair with bravado, they cheer him roundly.

Jerry sees the harm in this and goes to see Rocky before he starts the "last mile." He asks Rocky to do one thing—die yellow. Jerry points out how it may save thousands of boys from lives of crime. Rocky laughs and refuses.

As he enters the death chamber, Rocky suddenly changes his mind for his friend and goes to the chair screaming, wild-eyed, and full of fear. Later, the boys of the slums see little in their hero to idolize—little glory, less heroism.

Only Jerry and Laury know the truth.

*With Kay Francis and James Stephenson*

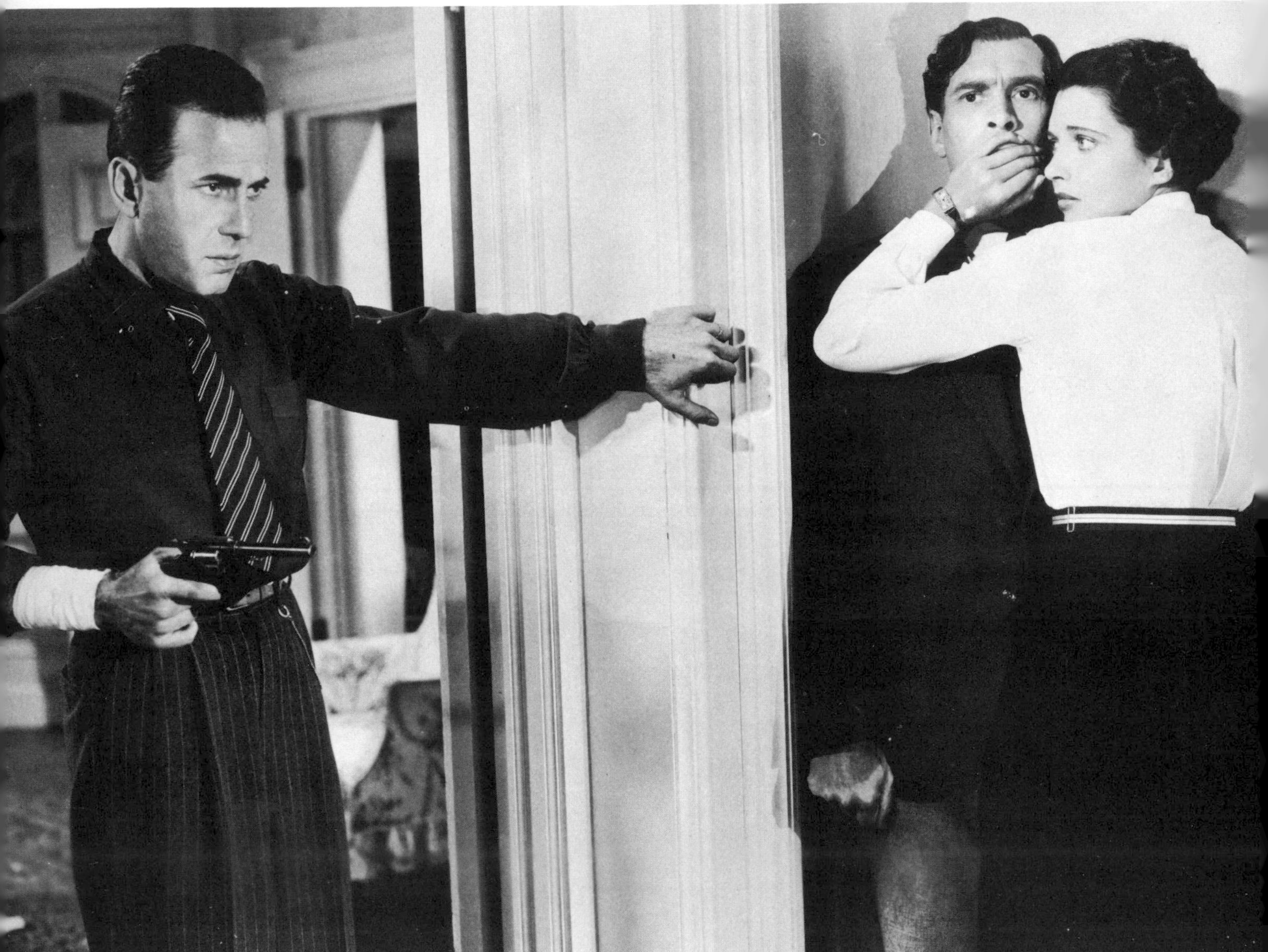

# King Of The Underworld

Carol and Niles Nelson are a splendid pair of surgeons. Man and wife, they are the star performers in the County Hospital surgical auditorium, before the ever-present medical student spectators. One day, when they operate on and save the life of a wounded gangster, there is another spectator in the gallery. Joe Gurney admires the skill of the man who has saved the criminal and, having Napoleonic complexes, decides, with no hesitation, to add Nelson to his "staff."

Nelson, whose penchant for betting is costly, is impatient for more income. He gets mixed up with the gangsters without Carol's knowledge, although she knows that something is wrong and that their marriage is going on the rocks.

Then one night she decides to spy on him. He is caught by the police in a raid on the gangsters' hide-out and killed. Carol is indicted for complicity. The jury that tries her disagrees, and she is freed, but the cloud on her name remains. Nearly ousted by the State Medical Board, she loses most of her patients. Determined to fight for complete exoneration from the charges and suspicions against her, she goes to a small country town where two of Gurney's men are held. They will not talk, but she hopes to make them when the trial comes up.

Meanwhile, she starts practice, but due to the opposition of her rival, the town doctor, gets no patients. Gurney arrives in town and frees the prisoners in a gun battle. Wounded in the fray, and accused of being a gangster, is the novelist Bill Forrest. Carol nurses him back to health, his identity is established, and together with Carol he corners the gangsters—he as a prisoner, she as their doctor.

Just in time to save herself, she blinds her dangerous "patients" with a chemical and turns them over to the police.

Directed by Lewis Seiler. Screenplay by George Bricker and Vincent Sherman. From a story by W. R. Burnett. Release date, January 1939. A Warner Brothers Picture.

| | |
|---|---|
| Joe Gurney | *Humphrey Bogart* |
| Carol Nelson | *Kay Francis* |
| Bill Forrest | *James Stephenson* |
| Niles Nelson | *John Eldredge* |
| Aunt Margaret | *Jessie Busley* |
| Dr. Sanders | *Arthur Aylesworth* |
| Sheriff | *Raymond Brown* |
| Mr. Ames | *Harland Tucker* |
| Mr. Robert | *Ralph Remley* |
| Eddie | *Charley Foy* |

# You Can't Get Away With Murder

Directed by Lewis Seiler. Associate Producer, Samuel Bischoff. Executive Producer, Hal B. Wallis. Screenplay by Robert Buckner, Don Ryan, and Kenneth Gamet. Based on the play, *Chalked Out*, by Warden Lewis E. Lawes and Jonathan Finn. Release date, May 1939. A Warner Brothers-First National Picture, 1939.

| | |
|---|---|
| Frank Wilson | *Humphrey Bogart* |
| Madge Stone | *Gale Page* |
| Johnnie Stone | *Billy Halop* |
| Attorney Carey | *John Litel* |
| Pop | *Henry Travers* |
| Fred Burke | *Harvey Stephens* |
| Scappa | *Harold Huber* |
| Red | *Joe Sawyer* |
| Smitty | *Joe Downing* |
| The Toad | *George E. Stone* |
| Principal Keeper | *Joseph King* |
| Warden | *Joseph Crehan* |
| Gas Station Attendant | *John Ridgely* |
| District Attorney | *Herbert Rawlinson* |

Johnnie Stone is a good kid until he starts running around with Frank Wilson, a smalltime crook, despite the ministrations of his sister, Madge Stone, and her fiancé, Fred Burke, a private patrolman.

Johnnie accompanies Wilson on several small jobs and then participates in a pawnshop robbery. He has taken along Burke's service revolver, which Wilson takes from him, and during the robbery the pawnbroker is shot dead—with the same gun. Next day Burke is arrested and charged with the murder, and Johnnie and Wilson are simultaneously arrested for some minor job and sent to prison.

Wilson fears the kid will crack and tell the truth to free his sister's boy friend. When he learns from "The Toad" that Pop, the prison librarian, has been working on the kid to tell the truth, he resolves to get Johnnie out of the way. He decides to take the kid on a break being planned by Scappa and Red, two gunmen, and kill him in the escape.

With the break set, Johnnie learns that Burke's appeal has been denied. Remorsefully he writes a full confession and contrives to drop it into Pop's cell. The break is started, the two gunmen are shot down, and Wilson and Johnnie hide among some freight cars, where they are found.

Wilson then shows Johnnie the confession which he had recovered from Pop's cell, and as the prison guard opens fire, he shoots down Johnnie. Then, just before he surrenders, he buries the note in the ground. He steps out and informs the warden Johnnie has been shot by the guards.

But Johnnie still has a spark of life left. He whispers out the story of the pawnbroker's death, and when the warden asks, "Have you any proof?" Johnny slowly unclenches his fist containing the confession he'd written to Pop.

He closes his eyes happily as the warden tells him that he's saved his sister's happiness.

*With Billy Halop*

JESSICA'S GIRL

# Dark Victory

A shadow of illness has fallen upon Judith Traherne, Long Island heiress, the darling of the set which plays hard but cleanly. Until now, she has had only one real love in her life—thoroughbred race horses.

Judith brushes off the signs of the illness, until her friends, who adore her, insist that she consult Dr. Fred Steele. An operation is called for, and although it is successful, a malignancy is found which indicates that Judith has but ten months to live.

Ann King, Judith's devoted secretary, learns from the doctor that Judith will soon die.

Judith, however, has fallen deeply and tenderly in love with the doctor and lets him know how she feels. The doctor loves her too—as do all around her: her impudent but likeable trainer of horses, Mickey, who is a magnificent physical specimen; Spec, her young, tongue-tied barn helper; her swain in the social set, Alec Strong. They all decide to keep the news of her certain death from her.

Accidentally she learns the truth, and fear and resentment lash her. She embarks on a wild whirl of cocktail parties.

Finally, when she visits the quarters of her impudent trainer near the stables one night, her everlasting courage snaps her out of her wild mood.

Contritely she goes to Ann, and they summon Dr. Steele. She tells them that she has wasted precious months—time that can never be replaced. She insists on her marriage to him at once. Together they go to a farm in Vermont.

Judith finds vast happiness in the simple and hearty life there. Every sunbeam, every walk through the pasture, every new curtain she puts up is a gem of pure delight. She imports bulbs from Holland, and, while planting them, rejoices in the mental picture of their beauty next year, when she will not be there to see the flowers. When her husband wishes to go with her at the end, she pledges him to carry on his work, for her sake. She has lived a lifetime of complete happiness since meeting him, she says. She reminds him that his talent belongs to all people.

Her call does come, and it is a calm and cheerful girl who accepts it. It is her victory over darkness.

Directed by Edmund Goulding. Executive Producer, Hal B. Wallis. Associate Producer, David Lewis. Screenplay by Casey Robinson. From the play by George Emerson Brewer, Jr. and Bertram Bloch. Release date, April 1939. A Warner Brothers-First National Picture.

| | |
|---|---|
| Judith Traherne | *Bette Davis* |
| Dr. Frederick Steele | *George Brent* |
| Michael O'Leary | *Humphrey Bogart* |
| Ann King | *Geraldine Fitzgerald* |
| Alec | *Ronald Reagan* |
| Dr. Parsons | *Henry Travers* |
| Carrie | *Cora Witherspoon* |
| Miss Wainwright | *Dorothy Peterson* |
| Martha | *Virginia Brissac* |
| Colonel Mantle | *Charles Richman* |
| Dr. Carter | *Herbert Rawlinson* |
| Dr. Driscoll | *Leonard Mudie* |
| Miss Dodd | *Fay Helm* |
| Lucy | *Lottie Williams* |

# The Oklahoma Kid

Directed by Lloyd Bacon. Associate Producer, Sam Bischoff. Executive Producer, Hal B. Wallis. Screenplay by Warren Duff, Robert Buckner, and Edward E. Paramore. From an original story by Edward E. Paramore and Wally Klein. Release date, March 1939. A Warner Brothers Picture.

| | |
|---|---|
| Jim Kincaid | *James Cagney* |
| Whip McCord | *Humphrey Bogart* |
| Jane Hardwick | *Rosemary Lane* |
| Judge Hardwick | *Donald Crisp* |
| Ned Kincaid | *Harvey Stephens* |
| John Kincaid | *Hugh Sothern* |
| Alec Martin | *Charles Middleton* |
| Doolin | *Edward Pawley* |
| Wes Handley | *Ward Bond* |
| Curley | *Lew Harvey* |
| Indian Jack Pasco | *Trevor Bardette* |
| Ringo | *John Miljan* |
| Judge Morgan | *Arthur Aylesworth* |
| Hotel Clerk | *Irving Bacon* |
| Keely | *Joe Devlin* |
| Sheriff | *Wade Boteler* |

The Cherokee Strip—1893—Oklahoma's fertile soil is opened to land-starved pioneers, lined up for miles awaiting the signal giving them land and new homes. At the sound of the gun, all rush forward to stake claims on a new life.

John Kincaid and his son, Ned, reach the site selected for their planned town, to find Whip McCord, notorious gambler, and his henchmen already on the ground. They have sneaked ahead of the starting gun. In exchange for the spot, they agree to give McCord the gambling and vice concession.

When gambling and lawlessness grow so rampant that the lawful elements decide to run John Kincaid for mayor and Ned for sheriff, to clean up the town, John is framed for murder by McCord and his gang.

News of the frame-up reaches the Oklahoma Kid, the West's most notorious outlaw. His real name is Jim Kincaid. Heading for the town, he meets Jane Hardwick, Ned's girl, and from her learns all the details. Then he confesses that he is John Kincaid's son, Ned's brother.

Tricking Judge Hardwick, an honest judge, out of town during the trial, McCord has John brought before one of his crooked judges. John is convicted and sentenced to hang.

The Kid storms into town and takes possession of the jail. Ned, now a U.S. marshal, and the Kid reach the saloon at the same time. The Kid slams through the door, both guns blazing. Ned is right behind him. A bullet from McCord's gun cuts Ned down. The Kid shoots it out with McCord, and after a terrific battle, kills him.

Ned dies a few moments later at Judge Hardwick's house. With his last breath he asks the judge to do all he can for his brother. The judge promises, and then Ned turns to the Kid and asks him to take care of Jane.

As his arm encircles Jane's waist, the Kid promises to hang up his guns and carry on where his and Ned's father stopped.

# The Return of Dr. X

Walter Garrett, an ambitious young reporter, gets the scoop of his life when he finds the dead body of actress Angela Merrova. But his glory is short-lived. The very next day, Miss Merrova, alive, but hiding an unearthly pallor under a black veil, visits Garrett's editor and announces the filing of a damage suit for $100,000.

Garrett is fired, but still believes he saw murder evidence. He determines to find out more about the actress, who has mysteriously quit the stage, and who makes midnight visits to the home of Dr. Francis Flegg, a brilliant but secretive blood specialist.

At about that time, all New York becomes increasingly alarmed by a series of strange murders. The slayings all seem to have been committed by a surgeon's deft knife, and the victims' bodies all prove to have been drained of blood. They also prove to have been blood-transfusion donors from Dr. Flegg's hospital. All the dead people were members of the same blood-type group.

Michael Rhodes, a young intern who assists Dr. Flegg and admires the elder man's genius, is Garrett's friend. He agrees to help Garrett fit the pieces of the murder puzzle together.

Garrett and Rhodes invade Dr. Flegg's laboratory, where they run into a clammy lab assistant named Dr. Cane. Cane's ghastly pallor and deep tones remind them at once of the wan actress, Merrova.

Dr. Flegg admits that he has been conducting experiments with synthetic blood, with which he has been able to restore life to rabbits and monkeys. Dr. Flegg astounds them when he tells them that he is on the verge of restoring life to humans. Then Dr. Cane is identified—he is the infamous Dr. Maurice Xavier who had been electrocuted a few years before, for murdering a patient upon whom he had been experimenting.

Shortly before Flegg himself dies at the hands of an assassin, he confesses that his synthetic blood has given rise to strange creatures who thirst for rich, warm human blood.

It is obvious that Dr. X has been committing the crimes that have terrorized the city, and finally Rhodes, Garrett, and Detective Kincaid rekill him in the marshes of New Jersey.

Directed by Vincent Sherman. Screenplay by Lee Katz. From a story by William J. Makin. Release date, December 1939. A Warner Brothers-First National Picture.

| | |
|---|---|
| Marshall Cane | *Humphrey Bogart* |
| Joan Vance | *Rosemary Lane* |
| Walter Garrett | *Wayne Morris* |
| Michael Rhodes | *Dennis Morgan* |
| Dr. Francis Flegg | *John Litel* |
| Angela Merrova | *Lya Lys* |
| Pinky | *Huntz Hall* |
| Detective Ray Kincaid | *Charles Wilson* |
| Miss Sweetman | *Vera Lewis* |
| Chairman | *Howard Hickman* |
| Undertaker | *Olin Howlin* |
| Guide | *Arthur Aylesworth* |
| Detective Sergeant Moran | *Jack Mower* |
| Hotel Manager | *Creighton Hale* |
| Rodgers | *John Ridgely* |
| Editor | *Joe Crehan* |
| Interne | *Glenn Langan* |
| Interne | *DeWolf Hopper* |

# The Roaring Twenties

Directed by Raoul Walsh. Associate Producer, Samuel Bischoff. Executive Producer, Hal B. Wallis. Screenplay by Jerry Wald, Richard Macaulay, and Robert Rossen. From an original story by Mark Hellinger. Release date, October 1939. A Warner Brothers Picture.

| | |
|---|---|
| Eddie Bartlett | *James Cagney* |
| Jean Whelan | *Priscilla Lane* |
| George Hally | *Humphrey Bogart* |
| Panama Smith | *Gladys George* |
| Lloyd Hart | *Jeffrey Lynn* |
| Danny Green | *Frank McHugh* |
| Nick Brown | *Paul Kelly* |
| Mrs. Sherman | *Elizabeth Risdon* |
| Henderson | *Ed Keane* |
| The Sergeant | *Joe Sawyer* |
| Michaels | *Joseph Crehan* |
| Masters | *George Meeker* |
| Judge | *John Hamilton* |
| First Detective | *Robert Elliott* |
| Second Detective | *Eddie Chandler* |
| Lefty | *Max Wagner* |
| Mrs. Gray | *Vera Lewis* |
| Narrator | *John Deering* |

Three buddies come home after World War I: Eddie Bartlett, a mechanic; George Hally, a saloonkeeper; and Lloyd Hart, a lawyer.

Eddie prospers as a bootlegger and retains Lloyd as his attorney. He meets and falls in love with Jean Whelan, a nice girl, working in the chorus of a show. He wants to marry her, but she has secretly fallen for Lloyd.

Eddie wants to branch out and highjacks a shipment of whiskey from a rival bootlegger. His old wartime friend, George, is in charge of the shipment. George leaves the rival gang and joins Eddie.

George discovers that Jean and Lloyd are in love and tells Eddie, but Eddie refuses to believe him. George and Eddie argue. George is jealous of Eddie's power and money. Their friendship ends.

Eddie loses everything in the Depression. He goes back to driving a cab. His only friend from the old days is Panama Smith, who operates a café. Almost five years pass, and Eddie meets Jean again. She has married Lloyd and they have a son. Lloyd is in the district attorney's office. Jean begs for Eddie's help. George, who has become a racket boss, has threatened Lloyd's life unless he agrees to quash the case against him. Eddie refuses to help her and she leaves sadly.

When Panama reasons with Eddie, tells him Jean must have a happy life to look forward to, he relents. Accompanied by Panama, he goes to George, but she waits outside when he enters George's apartment. Instead of agreeing not to harm Lloyd and Jean, George refuses. He traps Eddie and orders his men to take him for a ride. Through a trick, Eddie grabs a gun and kills George. Then, using one of the men as a shield, he attempts to fight his way through the other hoodlums, but is mortally wounded. The gun battle continues through the apartment and out into the street. As the police arrive, Eddie has attempted to find sanctuary in a church, but dies as he stumbles up the steps. The police ask Panama who Eddie is. She replies, with tears streaming down her cheeks, "He used to be a big shot."

# Invisible Stripes

Cliff Taylor and Chuck Martin are ex-cons. Cliff plans to go straight. Chuck, hard and tough, a seasoned criminal, goes back to his criminal way of life, joining Kruger and his gang.

When Cliff returns home, he finds that his girl doesn't want to marry him any more. She can never marry an ex-con. His brother, Tim, gets him a job, but he is fired when the foreman finds out that he has been in prison. He tries hard to find a job, but he finds nothing.

His brother wants to get married, but he doesn't have enough money. Cliff finds out that he has rolled a drunk, and he warns Tim against the life of crime. Cliff decides that the only way to keep Tim honest is to set him up in a business—and so he joins Chuck's gang.

Cliff gives Tim enough money to open a garage, and then Tim marries Peggy. He doesn't know that Cliff has become a criminal again; he thinks that he has an honest job. Cliff quits the mob as soon as there is enough money.

Chuck is wounded in a robbery and goes to Tim's garage to hide out. He tells Tim that Cliff was in on the holdup. Tim takes Chuck to a hide-out—Molly's apartment. When Tim returns to his garage, he is arrested.

At the police station, Cliff convinces Tim that he was not in on the robbery. He compels Tim to identify the gunman who came to his garage. Cliff also urges the police to keep Tim in protective custody.

Cliff goes to Molly's apartment to help Chuck escape. Three of the guilty gang follow him. As he reaches the hallway with the injured Chuck, the three gangsters appear. Cliff drags Chuck back to the apartment. The gangsters crash through, spraying the room with lead. Chuck is fatally shot and dies in Cliff's arms. Cliff is also mortally wounded as the police rush in and capture Kruger and Lefty. Cliff dies, a smile on his lips. At least he won't be going back to prison.

Directed by Lloyd Bacon. Associate Producer, Louis F. Edelman. Executive Producer, Hal B. Wallis. Screenplay by Warren Duff. From a story by Jonathan Finn. Based on the book by Warden Lewis E. Lawes. Release date, December 1939. A Warner Brothers-First National Picture.

| | |
|---|---|
| Cliff Taylor | *George Raft* |
| Peggy | *Jane Bryan* |
| Tim Taylor | *William Holden* |
| Chuck Martin | *Humphrey Bogart* |
| Mrs. Taylor | *Flora Robson* |
| Ed Kruger | *Paul Kelly* |
| Molly | *Lee Patrick* |
| Parole Officer Masters | *Henry O'Neill* |
| Tommy | *Frankie Thomas* |
| The Warden | *Moroni Olsen* |
| Sue | *Margot Stevenson* |
| Lefty | *Marc Lawrence* |
| Johnny | *Joseph Downing* |
| Jimmy | *Leo Gorcey* |
| Shrank | *William Haade* |
| Old Peter | *Tully Marshall* |

*With William Holden*

# Virginia City

Directed by Michael Curtiz. Associate
Producer, Robert Fellows. Executive
Producer, Hal B. Wallis. Screenplay by Robert
Buckner. Release date, March 1940. A
Warner Brothers-First National Picture.

| | |
|---|---|
| Kerry Bradford | *Errol Flynn* |
| Julia Haynes | *Miriam Hopkins* |
| Vance Irby | *Randolph Scott* |
| John Murrell | *Humphrey Bogart* |
| Mr. Upjohn | *Frank McHugh* |
| Moose | *Alan Hale* |
| Marblehead | *Guinn "Big Boy" Williams* |
| Major Drewery | *Douglass Dumbrille* |
| Cameron | *John Litel* |
| Armistead | *Moroni Olsen* |
| Cobby | *Dickie Jones* |
| Union Soldier | *Frank Wilcox* |
| Gaylord | *Russell Simpson* |
| Abraham Lincoln | *Victor Kilian* |
| Jefferson Davis | *Charles Middleton* |

In the final stages of the Civil War, Kerry Bradford, a Union officer, is in a Confederate prison. With other prisoners he is digging a tunnel to escape.

At the same time, Julia Haynes, a dance-hall entertainer, is working as a Confederate spy. She has a plan to refinance the sagging Confederacy by smuggling five million dollars in gold bullion donated by wealthy Southern sympathizers out of Virginia City.

She reveals her plan to Vance Irby, commandant of the Confederate prison. Vance tells the plan to Jefferson Davis, who assigns Vance to carry it out. Meanwhile, Kerry and his friends escape from the prison and return to Union headquarters. General Hooker sends Kerry to stop the smuggling.

On the stagecoach, Kerry and Julia meet and fall in love, each ignorant of the other's secret mission. They also meet Murrell, a notorious guerilla, who tries to rob them. He is wounded, but manages to escape. In Virginia City, Vance is secretly removing the gold concealed in covered wagons.

That night Kerry and Vance meet and recognize each other. Kerry is certain that Vance is removing the gold, and Vance knows Kerry is there to prevent it.

The town is searched by Union troops, but Vance is gone. He is hiding at the home of Dr. Cameron. While there, the wounded Murrell is brought in. Vance makes a deal with Murrell. He offers $10,000 if Murrell and his men attack the Union garrison and divert them so that the gold can be removed from the city.

Kerry is captured and hates Julia because she has tricked him. The gold train escapes into the desert, but Kerry escapes.

Murrell is not satisfied. He trails the wagons, intent on capturing the gold. He attacks the Southerners, but Kerry returns and fights side-by-side with Vance. Murrell is driven off, but Vance is shot, and Kerry takes command. Murrell renews his attack, and Kerry kills Murrell as the Union troops arrive on the scene. Kerry is returned to Virginia City for court-martial.

In the midst of the court-martial the war ends. Virginia City goes wild. Southerners embrace Northerners—and Kerry embraces Julia.

# It All Came True

The last time Maggie Ryan heard from Sarah Jane, her daughter, Sarah Jane had a new job as an entertainer in a night club. Mrs. Taylor, plump and sixtyish, Maggie Ryan's partner in a unique boardinghouse, has not heard from her musician son, Tommy, in almost five years. Mrs. Taylor has woven stories about him, saying that someday he would return rich and famous.

The Ryan-Taylor boardinghouse, a four-story brownstone affair, was left to the two old ladies by their mistress. The place is still furnished in the Victorian style of forty years ago. Rattling around in the mansion are four ancient boarders: Miss Flint, Mr. Salmon, Mr. Van Diver, and The Great Boldini. None of the boarders pays rent, but somehow Maggie and Mrs. Taylor keep the old place going.

One night there is a scuffle on the front porch, and Sarah Jane Ryan has come home, triumphant over the unhappy masher. Home, too, a few nights later, comes Tommy Taylor, and with Tommy is a mysterious stranger, a "Mr. Grasselli," who immediately engages a room, leaving orders that he must never be disturbed. Grasselli actually is Chips Maguire, a gambler and a night club owner, for whom Tommy has been working as a piano player on the promise that Grasselli will get some of Tommy's music published. Grasselli has just been involved in a gangland killing. He forces Tommy to bring him to Tommy's old home as a hideaway. Weeks pass. Sarah Jane and Tommy continue their childhood fights and quarrels, both refusing to recognize the love they feel underneath.

Grasselli gradually softens under the ministrations of Maggie and Mrs. Taylor, and even keeps his temper when one day he is recognized as Chips Maguire by Sarah Jane. When money is needed to save the banks from foreclosing on the old house, Maguire decides to transform the old house, as is, into a Gay Nineties night club. This is done, and the place is a huge success, with Sarah Jane and Tommy the hits of the show. Finally, Grasselli is arrested.

Instead of involving Tommy in the original shooting, Maguire gives Sarah Jane and Tommy his blessings and wishes them every happiness.

Directed by Lewis Seiler. Associate Producer, Mark Hellinger. Executive Producer, Hal B. Wallis. Screenplay by Michael Fessier and Lawrence Kimble. From a novel by Louis Bromfield. Release date, April 1940. A Warner Brothers-First National Picture.

| | |
|---|---|
| Sarah Jane Ryan | *Ann Sheridan* |
| Tommy Taylor | *Jeffrey Lynn* |
| Grasselli (Chips Maguire) | *Humphrey Bogart* |
| Miss Flint | *Zasu Pitts* |
| Maggie Ryan | *Una O'Connor* |
| Mrs. Taylor | *Jessie Busley* |
| Mr. Roberts | *John Litel* |
| Rene Salmon | *Grant Mitchell* |
| The Great Boldini | *Felix Bressart* |
| Henri Pepi de Bordeaux | *Charles Judels* |
| Mr. Van Diver | *Brandon Tynan* |
| Mr. Prendergast | *Howard Hickman* |
| Monks | *Herbert Vigran* |

With: *Tommy Reilly, The Elderbloom Chorus, Bender and Daum, White and Stanley, The Lady Killers' Quartet.*

*With Ann Sheridan*

# Brother Orchid

Directed by Lloyd Bacon. Executive Producer, Hal B. Wallis. Associate Producer, Mark Hellinger. Screenplay by Earl Baldwin. Based on a story by Richard Connell. Release date, June 1940. A Warner Brothers-First National Picture.

| | |
|---|---|
| Little John Sarto | *Edward G. Robinson* |
| Flo Addams | *Ann Sothern* |
| Jack Buck | *Humphrey Bogart* |
| Brother Superior | *Donald Crisp* |
| Clarence Fletcher | *Ralph Bellamy* |
| Willie the Knife | *Allen Jenkins* |
| Brother Wren | *Charles D. Brown* |
| Brother Goodwin | *Cecil Kellaway* |
| Philadelphia Powell | *Morgan Conway* |
| Mugsy O'Day | *Richard Lane* |
| Red Martin | *Paul Guilfoyle* |
| Texas Pearson | *John Ridgely* |
| Brother MacEwen | *Joseph Crehan* |
| Brother MacDonald | *Wilfred Lucas* |
| Curley Matthews | *Tom Tyler* |
| Buffalo Burns | *Dick Wessell* |
| Pattonville Superintendent | *Granville Bates* |
| French Frank | *Paul Phillips* |
| Al Muller | *Don Rowan* |
| Fifi | *Nanette Vallon* |
| Turkey Malone | *Tim Ryan* |
| Handsome Harry | *Joe Caites* |
| Dopey Perkins | *Pat Gleason* |
| Joseph | *Tommy Baker* |

Little John Sarto, a big-time racketeer, is convinced that there is no future in the rackets. He decides to quit and names Jack Buck as his successor. His girl friend, Flo, is heartbroken.

Little John goes to Europe, but finds it a little rich for his blood, and after five years he returns to New York. He wants to take his place once again at the head of the syndicate.

Buck tells Little John that he is through and had better get out of town. He is heartbroken. He looks up Flo and finds that she is going steady with Clarence, a rich alfalfa farmer from the Midwest.

Little John gets in touch with Willie the Knife, the only member of his old mob to remain faithful to him. He drives over to the hospital where Willie is hiding out. He starts to organize a new mob in direct competition with Buck. Philadelphia Powell and Buck are set to rub out Little John. They lead him to a nice quiet spot in the woods, but he trips them, and makes a mad dash through the dark for safety. They manage to wing him in the shoulder, but he keeps going, and finally collapses.

He wakes to hear birds singing and an organ pealing in the distance. He thinks he's in heaven, but it's a monastery, and the brothers welcome him as one of themselves.

He joins in the simple life of the monastery, helping the brothers cultivate their flowers, which they sell in town for the benefit of the poor. They dub him Brother Orchid.

One day the truck comes back from the city still loaded with the flowers—they cannot sell them because they don't belong to the protective association, run by Buck.

Little John determines to do something about it and also settle scores with Flo, who he thinks double-crossed him. Meanwhile, thinking him dead, she has agreed to marry Clarence, and he has brought all his friends from the Midwest for the event.

Little John shows up, something of an apparition in his monk's cassock and shaven pate. Flo cancels the wedding. Then Little John gets Clarence and his friends, and they descend on Buck and his mob. It proves quite a party.

The forces of right prevail, though somewhat the worse for wear. Little John now realizes that Clarence deserves Flo more than he does and bows out of the picture.

It is the end of Little John Sarto, the real beginning of Brother Orchid.

*With Edward G. Robinson*

*With
George
Raft
and
Ann
Sheridan*

*With
Gale
Page*

# They Drive By Night

Joe and Paul Fabrini are independent truck drivers, and by working night and day they manage to keep ahead of Mr. Farnsworth, who continually hounds them for the back payments.

One night, in a driving rainstorm, they swerve to avoid an accident, and the wheel of their truck breaks. At Barney's Café they meet Cassie, a high-spirited, red-haired waitress.

Later that night they stop to give a hitchhiker a ride, and it turns out to be Cassie. She is broke, refuses Joe's offer to put her up in an apartment, but finally does accept his offer of a cheap hotel room. The next morning Joe meets Ed Carlsen, the owner of a big trucking fleet, and his wife, Lana. Lana is infatuated with Joe, but her affection is not returned.

The Fabrinis have a streak of luck and pay off Farnsworth. Then Paul has a terrific crash. Paul loses an arm; their truck and money are lost; and Joe's only out is to accept Carlsen's standing offer of a job.

Lana continues to force herself on Joe, but he keeps his distance. Later that night, when Lana and her husband return home from a party, Carlsen is drunk. She leaves him in the garage, the car motor running.

The authorities accept Carlsen's death as accidental. Lana calls Joe to her home. She asks him to become her partner. The company prospers under Joe's management, but Lana, who hopes to find the path to her desires clear now, finds him more distant than ever. When she learns about Cassie and meets her, she goes almost literally crazy.

Wildly desperate, she throws up the murder of Carlsen, accusing Joe of making her commit the crime. She ends up in the district attorney's office, and Fabrini is arrested for murder.

All the circumstantial evidence points to his guilt. Even the testimony of his friends unwittingly compromises him.

But when Lana herself takes the stand, and when Joe's cold, accusing eyes meet hers and hold them, she goes completely to pieces. Because she is obviously insane, Joe is freed.

Directed by Raoul Walsh. Associate Producer, Mark Hellinger. Executive Producer, Hal B. Wallis. Screenplay by Jerry Wald and Richard Macaulay. From a novel by A. I. Bezzerides. Release date, August 1940. A Warner Brothers-First National Picture.

| | |
|---|---|
| Joe Fabrini | *George Raft* |
| Cassie Hartley | *Ann Sheridan* |
| Lana Carlsen | *Ida Lupino* |
| Paul Fabrini | *Humphrey Bogart* |
| Pearl Fabrini | *Gale Page* |
| Ed Carlsen | *Alan Hale* |
| Irish McGurn | *Roscoe Karns* |
| Harry McNamara | *John Litel* |
| George Rondolos | *George Tobias* |
| District Attorney | *Henry O'Neill* |

# High Sierra

Directed by Raoul Walsh. Associate Producer, Mark Hellinger. Executive Producer, Hal B. Wallis. Screenplay by John Huston and W. R. Burnett. From a novel by W. R. Burnett. Release date, January 1941. A Warner Brothers-First National Picture.

| | |
|---|---|
| Marie | *Ida Lupino* |
| Roy Earle | *Humphrey Bogart* |
| Babe | *Alan Curtis* |
| Red | *Arthur Kennedy* |
| Velma | *Joan Leslie* |
| Doc Banton | *Henry Hull* |
| Pa | *Henry Travers* |
| Healy | *Jerome Cowan* |
| Mrs. Baughman | *Minna Gombell* |
| Jack Kranmer | *Barton MacLane* |
| Ma | *Elizabeth Risdon* |
| Louis Mendoza | *Cornel Wilde* |
| Big Mac | *Donald MacBride* |
| Mr. Baughmam | *Paul Harvey* |
| Blonde | *Isabel Jewell* |
| Algernon | *Willie Best* |
| Ed | *Spencer Charters* |
| Pfiffer | *George Meeker* |
| Art | *Robert Strange* |
| Lon Preiser | *John Eldredge* |
| Announcer | *Sam Hayes* |
| Pard | *Zero* |

Roy Earle, the last of the Dillinger gang, is released from prison, through the efforts of Big Mac, to head a mob that will rob the swank Tropico Inn. With Kranmer, Big Mac's henchman, Roy starts off for the mountaintop camp that will serve as a hide-out. On the way they meet Ma and Pa Goodhue and their crippled granddaughter, Velma.

At the camp Roy meets Babe and Red, his young associates, Marie, a dance-hall girl, and Pard, a friendly dog. Mendoza, another gang member, is their contact at the inn.

Roy meets Big Mac in Los Angeles and while there arranges for an operation for Velma. The operation is a success, but Roy discovers that Velma already has a lover. Roy returns sadly to the camp.

Mendoza tells them that there is a fortune at the inn, and Roy sends Red and Babe to the resort in one car, while Roy, Marie, and the dog go in another car. A watchman interrupts the robbery. Roy shoots him. They escape. Red and Babe crash and burn to death in the car. The police capture Mendoza.

Marie and Roy flee to Los Angeles, where Roy discovers Big Mac dead and Kranmer waiting for him. Roy and Kranmer exchange shots. Roy is wounded, but Kranmer falls dead.

Los Angeles proves too hot for the gunman, and the fence says that it will take time to dispose of the jewels. Newspaper headlines reveal that Mendoza has described Roy, Marie, and the dog to the police. Roy puts Marie on an eastbound bus with Pard, but he is recognized while robbing a shop to replenish his funds, and finds his desperate flight halted on one of the high mountain passes.

Hearing a broadcast of the police chase, Marie returns to the scene of Roy's last stand in the mountains. She is unable to get past the police lines, but Pard jumps from her arms and scampers up the big boulders to Roy's stronghold. Hearing the dog bark, Roy runs out calling Marie's name, and a shot from a concealed rifleman ends his career. Marie weeps bitterly as she is led away.

# The Wagons Roll At Night

Nick Coster, hard and cynical, is the owner of a third-rate carnival. His sister, Mary, is his one soft spot. He keeps her sheltered from everything, on a farm in a nearby state. He is in love with Flo Lorraine, "Madame Florina," the fortuneteller with the outfit.

At Hentyville, Coster's Original Coney Island Carnival gets into trouble. It happens because Hoffman, the lion tamer, gets drunk. One of the beasts escapes from the arena and heads for town.

Matt Varney, towheaded, grinning, strictly a Hentyville product, is waiting on a customer in the general store. A customer faints, but Matt, too easygoing to be alarmed, grabs a pitchfork, backs the lion into a corner, and holds it there until help arrives.

As a result, Nick offers Matt a job with the carnival. Matt works with Hoffman in the lion act and proves to be a sensational draw. As time goes on, Matt learns, improves, and soon is better with the lions than the drunken Hoffman. Eventually, Hoffman is fired; Matt gets the job and feature billing with the show: Varney of the Lions.

Matt meets Mary and falls in love with her, but Nick finds out and ends the brief romance. He drags Matt back to the carnival.

Nick plans to get rid of Matt. He literally forces the boy to work Caesar, the mad lion, into the act. Flo learns of this and rushes to the farm to get Mary's help. But they get to the show grounds too late. Matt is already working Caesar in the ring. It is a terrific battle between man and untamed beast. The audience is limp. But eventually Matt comes out of the cage alive.

As he enters his dressing room, he is confronted by Hoffman, the drunken ex-trainer, now a homicidal maniac. Hoffman is obsessed by the idea that Matt is the one who took away his job.

But just as Hoffman draws a gun and prepares to fire, Nick Coster enters. Without drawing his gun from his pocket, Nick shoots Hoffman and kills him. But Nick receives a fatal wound before Hoffman falls.

As Nick lies dying he asks forgiveness of Flo, Mary, and Matt. He wishes lifelong happiness for his sister and Varney of the Lions.

Directed by Ray Enright. Associate Producer, Harlan Thompson. Screenplay by Fred Niblo, Jr. and Barry Trivers. Suggested by a story by Francis Wallace. Release date, April 1941. A Warner Brothers-First National Picture.

| | |
|---|---|
| Nick Coster | *Humphrey Bogart* |
| Flo Lorraine | *Sylvia Sidney* |
| Matt Varney | *Eddie Albert* |
| Mary Coster | *Joan Leslie* |
| Hoffman The Great | *Sig Rumann* |
| Doc | *Cliff Clark* |
| Snapper | *Charley Foy* |
| Tex | *Frank Wilcox* |
| Arch | *John Ridgely* |
| Mrs. Williams | *Clara Blandick* |
| Mr. Williams | *Aldrich Bowker* |
| Gus | *Garry Owen* |
| Bundy | *Jack Mower* |
| Wally | *Frank Mayo* |

# The Maltese Falcon

Directed by John Huston. Associate Producer, Henry Blanke. Executive Producer, Hal B. Wallis. Screenplay by John Huston. Based on the novel by Dashiell Hammett. Release date, October 1941. A Warner Brothers-First National Picture.

| | |
|---|---|
| Sam Spade | *Humphrey Bogart* |
| Brigid O'Shaughnessy | *Mary Astor* |
| Iva Archer | *Gladys George* |
| Joel Cairo | *Peter Lorre* |
| Lt. of Detectives Dundy | *Barton MacLane* |
| Effie Perine | *Lee Patrick* |
| Kasper Gutman | *Sydney Greenstreet* |
| Detective Tom Polhaus | *Ward Bond* |
| Miles Archer | *Jerome Cowan* |
| Wilmer | *Elisha Cook, Jr.* |
| Luke | *James Burke* |
| Frank Richman | *Murray Alper* |
| Bryan | *John Hamilton* |

Sam Spade, private investigator with ice water in his veins, has just learned that his partner, Archer, has been murdered while trailing a man named Thursby. Soon after, Spade is informed that Thursby has also been murdered.

Brigid O'Shaughnessy had hired Archer to follow Thursby. She now says that she is in danger of losing her life and retains Spade for an additional $500 (which he forces out of her) to protect her name and interests.

It is only a few hours later that a strange man visits Spade's office. The stranger named Cairo offers Spade $5,000 to find him a certain statuette, a black porcelain falcon.

Brigid joins with Spade to find the falcon for Cairo. Two others enter the case: Mr. Gutman, a huge man with something obscene about him; and a boy called Wilmer. Wilmer is Gutman's gun boy. Gutman is more generous than Cairo. He offers Spade $50,000 for the falcon.

Presently Spade learns the nature of the mysterious falcon. It is supposed to be worth a fabulous fortune, encrusted with jewels, once a gift of the Knights of Malta to Charles of Spain. Spade learns that it is to be delivered to Brigid by the captain of a boat arriving from the Orient.

Effie, the secretary, is talking to Spade when the door bursts open and a badly wounded man staggers into the room carrying a bundle. The man dies. He is the captain Spade has expected. Spade opens the package. In it is the Maltese Falcon. Spade hides the falcon in the locker room of a bus station and goes to look for Brigid and the others.

He finds them together in his apartment. They agree to turn Wilmer over to the police as the killer of Archer, Thursby, and the captain. Spade is to get $10,000 for the statue plus Brigid and her love.

But the Maltese Falcon proves to be a fake. The real falcon is yet to be found.

The police have Cairo, Gutman, and Wilmer. Spade proves that Wilmer killed Thursby and the captain. Wilmer adds another to his list. He kills Gutman before he can be stopped.

And Spade turns Brigid over to the police for the murder of Archer, his partner. Spade turns the Maltese Falcon over to his friend the detective.

# All Through The Night

Gloves Donahue is a onetime mobster who now devotes himself to gambling to support himself, his mother, and the remnants of his gang in the style to which they're accustomed. Directly or indirectly, this philanthropic citizen also supports a good many other people.

There is, for example, Mr. Miller, the old baker. Gloves keeps him going by forcing a large number of cafés to stock Mr. Miller's excellent cheesecake.

Returning from a ball game, Gloves finds that Mr. Miller has been murdered. At the same time Gloves meets a mysterious young woman. She seems to have some connection with the mystery. He learns that the mystery woman, Leda Hamilton, sings at a café owned by a onetime rival mob boss, Callahan.

Gloves goes to the café to hear Leda sing, and he sees her taken away by a character named Pepi and witnesses the dying gasps of one of Callahan's gorillas, who says "Fivers" shot him.

While Gloves dodges the police, who think he killed Callahan's man, he trails Pepi and Leda to an old warehouse. There he discovers many other men, enemy agents—"Fivers"—fifth columnists.

Gloves leaves the warehouse and enters an auction house. The auctioneer, Ebbing, and his assistant, Madame, are also enemy agents. Gloves tries to choke Ebbing into saying what they have done with Leda.

Leda, he learns, is in the power of the enemy because her father is being held hostage. Gloves also learns that the agents plan to dynamite a ship in New York harbor by means of a speedboat. Gloves and his aides start out to prevent this and to snatch Leda from her captors.

Near the waterfront, Gloves finds a "Fiver" meeting in progress. He attends, posing as a spy who has come to report. He is about to be captured when he is saved by Callahan and his men.

Only one agent has escaped, Ebbing, and Gloves chases him. Ebbing and Gloves battle on the explosive-carrying torpedo boat, and Gloves falls into the water. The out-of-control boat hits an anchored barge and there is a mighty explosion.

That is the end of Ebbing and the "Fivers" plot.

Back on shore Gloves finds a royal reception. Leda waits for him with open arms.

Directed by Vincent Sherman. Executive Producer, Hal B. Wallis. Associate Producer, Jerry Wald. Screenplay by Leonard Spigelgass and Edwin Gilbert. From a story by Leonard Q. Ross and Leonard Spigelgass. Release date, January 1942. A Warner Brothers-First National Picture.

| | |
|---|---|
| Gloves Donahue | *Humphrey Bogart* |
| Ebbing | *Conrad Veidt* |
| Leda Hamilton | *Kaaren Verne* |
| Mrs. Donahue | *Jane Darwell* |
| Barney | *Frank McHugh* |
| Pepi | *Peter Lorre* |
| Madame | *Judith Anderson* |
| Sunshine | *William Demarest* |
| Starchy | *Jackie C. Gleason* |
| Waiter | *Phil Silvers* |
| Spats Hunter | *Wally Ford* |
| Marty Callahan | *Barton MacLane* |
| Joe Denning | *Edward Brophy* |
| Steindorff | *Martin Kosleck* |
| Annabelle | *Jean Ames* |
| Mr. Miller | *Ludwig Stossell* |
| Mrs. Miller | *Irene Seidner* |
| Forbes | *James Burke* |
| Smitty | *Ben Welden* |
| Anton | *Hans Schumm* |
| Sage | *Charles Cane* |
| Spence | *Frank Sully* |
| Deacon | *Sam McDaniel* |

# The Big Shot

Directed by Lewis Seiler. Screenplay by Bertram Millhauser, Abem Finkel, and Daniel Fuchs. Release date, June 1942. A Warner Brothers-First National Picture.

| | |
|---|---|
| Duke Berne | *Humphrey Bogart* |
| Lorna Fleming | *Irene Manning* |
| George Anderson | *Richard Travis* |
| Ruth Carter | *Susan Peters* |
| Martin Fleming | *Stanley Ridges* |
| Warden Booth | *Minor Watson* |
| Dancer | *Chick Chandler* |
| Frenchy | *Joseph Downing* |
| Sandor | *Howard da Silva* |
| Quinto | *Murray Alper* |
| Faye | *Roland Drew* |
| Tim | *John Ridgely* |
| Toohey | *Joseph King* |
| Judge | *John Hamilton* |
| Mrs. Booth | *Virginia Brissac* |
| Sarto | *William Edmunds* |
| Mrs. Miggs | *Virginia Sale* |
| Kat | *Ken Christy* |
| Rusty | *Wallace Scott* |

Duke Berne, double-crosser, gangster, and three-time loser, once a big shot, is down and out. He comes across Frenchy and Faye, smalltime thugs, in a cheap café. First they slap Duke around, but then offer him the chance to take part in a robbery. Duke declines—his nerve is gone. They promise the protection of famed criminal lawyer Martin Fleming.

Berne resolves to go through with the holdup in order to get money. Lorna, Fleming's wife, begs him not to, but Duke returns to the café and takes charge of the plot.

But on the night it is to take place, Duke fails to show up. Frenchy and Faye try to go through with it and bungle the job, but manage to escape. The police suspect Duke, show his picture to a woman who witnessed the robbery, and badger her into identifying Duke. After a swift trial, Duke is convicted and sentenced to life.

Determined to escape, Duke falls in with an ex-hoofer, and the pair of them plot a break on the night of the annual prison show. They hide their guns and tools in the sawdust back of a dummy used in a comic sequence, and in the midst of the show, Duke douses the lights and they start out. The dancer is killed, but Duke gets over the wall after killing a guard.

Anderson, who helped stage the show, is charged with the murder of the guard.

Then Duke and Lorna run away together, hoping to make it to Canada, where they can start life anew. On the way, the police spot them, and in a desperate chase, Duke escapes. But Lorna is shot and dies in the car beside Duke.

Before he gives himself up, Duke goes to Fleming's apartment. He feels that Fleming has murdered Lorna by squealing to the police. And when he confronts Fleming, he declines all the lawyer's offers of money and protection. But as he starts to shoot, Fleming flips the lights out, draws his own gun, and fires. Duke is mortally wounded, but he empties his revolver at Fleming and kills him.

Before he dies, he calls State Prison and tells them that he killed the guard, and that the man they have charged with the crime is really innocent. Then Duke dies.

*With
Irene
Manning*

# Across The Pacific

Dismissed from the service by a court-martial verdict, Rick Leland is a lonely, disgraced man. He goes to the N.Y.K. Japanese steamship company, where he books passage on the freighter *Genoa Maru*, bound for Yokohama by way of New York, Panama, and Honolulu.

That night, as the *Genoa Maru* sails, Rick introduces himself to Alberta Marlow, an attractive young woman. Rick also encounters another passenger, Dr. Lorenz, who identifies himself as a sociologist. Dr. Lorenz reveals his affinity for the Japanese and points out that they are a "wonderful, greatly misunderstood" people.

Later, Rick meets Lorenz again. Rick admits that he is broke and also that he has been dishonorably discharged—at the same time displaying an unusually detailed knowledge of U.S. military affairs.

When the ship docks in New York, Rick meets Colonel Hart of the U.S. Army, who greets him warmly. From the conversation it becomes apparent that Rick is actually in the Army secret service and that Dr. Lorenz is the man he is after.

Back on the *Genoa Maru*, Rick saves Lorenz's life when he is attacked by a Filipino assassin. The following day Lorenz approaches Rick with a deal whereby Rick will be well paid for certain information about military installations near the Panama Canal. Rick accepts some money with the promise of more when the information is delivered.

In Panama, Rick makes contact with another American agent. Alberta accuses Rick of complicity with the Lorenz gang and is about to tell him something when she disappears after going to make a phone call. Rick searches for her and then goes back to his own room, where he finds Lorenz waiting for him. Lorenz has learned that Rick is an agent.

Rick escapes after learning that Dr. Lorenz plans to blow up the Gatun Locks of the Panama Canal with torpedoes from a Japanese-piloted plane.

Rick goes to a clearing where he can see a plane being loaded with torpedoes. Rick moves closer, draws a bead on one of the torpedoes, and fires. As the plane explodes, it virtually disappears. Rick captures Lorenz on the spot.

Directed by John Huston. Produced by Jerry Wald and Jack Saper. Screenplay by Richard Macaulay. From the *Saturday Evening Post* serial by Robert Carson. Release date, September 1942. A Warner Brothers-First National Picture.

| | |
|---|---|
| Rick Leland | *Humphrey Bogart* |
| Alberta Marlow | *Mary Astor* |
| Dr. Lorenz | *Sydney Greenstreet* |
| A. V. Smith | *Charles Halton* |
| Joe Totsuiko | *Sen Yung* |
| Sugi | *Roland Got* |
| Sam Wing On | *Lee Tung Foo* |
| Captain Morrison | *Frank Wilcox* |
| Colonel Hart | *Paul Stanton* |
| Canadian Major | *Lester Matthews* |
| Court-Martial President | *John Hamilton* |
| Unidentified Man | *Tom Stevenson* |
| Captain Harkness | *Roland Drew* |
| Dan Morton | *Monte Blue* |
| Captain Higoto | *Chester Gan* |
| First Officer Miyuma | *Richard Loo* |
| Steamship Office Clerk | *Keye Luke* |
| T. Oki | *Kam Tong* |
| Chief Engineer Mitsuko | *Spencer Chan* |
| A Filipino Assassin | *Rudy Robles* |

# Casablanca

Directed by Michael Curtiz. Screenplay by Julius J. and Philip G. Epstein. From a play by Murray Burnett and Joan Alison. Release date, January 1943. A Hal B. Wallis Production. A Warner Brothers-First National Picture.

| | |
|---|---|
| Rick | *Humphrey Bogart* |
| Ilsa Lund | *Ingrid Bergman* |
| Victor Laszlo | *Paul Henreid* |
| Captain Louis Renault | *Claude Rains* |
| Major Strasser | *Conrad Veidt* |
| Senor Ferrari | *Sydney Greenstreet* |
| Ugarte | *Peter Lorre* |
| Carl, a Waiter | *S. Z. Sakall* |
| Yvonne | *Madeleine LeBeau* |
| Sam | *Dooley Wilson* |
| Annina Brandel | *Joy Page* |
| Berger | *John Qualen* |
| Sascha, a Bartender | *Leonid Kinskey* |
| Dark European | *Curt Bois* |
| Jan | *Helmut Dantine* |
| Croupier | *Marcel Dalio* |
| Singer | *Corinna Mura* |
| Mr. Leuchtag | *Ludwig Stossel* |
| Mrs. Leuchtag | *Ilka Gruning* |
| Arab Vendor | *Frank Puglia* |
| Abdul | *Dan Seymour* |

Casablanca is a way station out of war-torn Europe. Here those with money or influence or luck obtain passports and scurry to Lisbon, and then to the Americas. The others wait in Casablanca.

Overhead a Nazi plane circles down, and Major Heinrich Strasser arrives in Casablanca to investigate the death of two German couriers who have been murdered for their letters of transit. He goes into conference with Captain Louis Renault, the prefect of police, a gay but shrewd man with a penchant for money and pretty faces.

Renault assures Strasser that the murderer will be captured that night at Rick's Café, the center of everything that happens in Casablanca.

Rick is an American who, after being thrown over in Paris after the great love affair of his life, now runs the café and gambling hot spot.

Ugarte, a runner in the black market, asks Rick to hide two documents for him. The letters of transit. Rick agrees, dropping the papers into the small piano played by Sam, the entertainer at the café.

Renault arrests Ugarte, but he tries to escape and is killed. Then Victor Laszlo and his wife, Ilsa, enter the café. He is the head of the underground, and she is the girl that Rick loved in Paris.

They claim Ugarte's documents. Renault and Strasser are determined not to let Laszlo out of Casablanca. Ilsa comes to see Rick after hours, but he is bitter, and Ilsa leaves in tears.

Rick tries to find out the real value of the letters of transit from Ferrari, head of the black market. His café is ransacked.

Laszlo offers Rick a fortune for the letters of transit, but Rick refuses. When asked why, Rick tells him to ask his wife.

Ilsa tries to persuade Rick that Laszlo's work is vastly important, that he must have the documents to continue. Then she explains why she had to leave him in Paris, that Laszlo, her husband whom she had assumed to be dead, had returned.

Understanding now, Rick forces Renault to phone the airport and gives instructions for the safe passage from Casablanca of both Laszlo and Ilsa.

Strasser is shot in the ensuing battle, but Laszlo and Ilsa make a safe getaway.

*With Ingrid Bergman*

*With Claude Rains*

121

Joe Rossi is the first mate aboard an American tanker in the early days of the war. One foggy night the skipper of the ship, Captain Jarvis, orders the watch doubled. The words are hardly out of Jarvis's mouth when a torpedo hits square in the engine room and the ship has to be abandoned. The lifeboat is lowered, and after fifteen days, the men are picked up by a destroyer.

Back in New York after the ordeal, Joe meets and marries Pearl O'Neill, but even before the honeymoon, Captain Jarvis gets a new ship, the *Seawitch*, and once again Rossi signs on as first mate.

The *Seawitch* joins a task force in the North Atlantic, which loses contact in the fog. Captain Jarvis spots the periscope of a U-boat and orders the course of the *Seawitch* changed, to lure the sub away from the rest of the convoy.

Through the long, black night during which the U-boat keeps out of range, Joe tries to think of a way to shake the sub. He orders absolute silence on board, and by morning the sub is gone.

Almost immediately unidentified planes are sighted. They are German bombers, and the youthful gun crew goes into action. During the bombing, Captain Jarvis is wounded, and Rossi takes command of the ship. Several bombers are downed, and the attack is finally beaten off.

But no sooner have the planes left and the dead been buried, than the sub returns. A torpedo splits the *Seawitch*. Rossi realizes that if the sub thinks that the *Seawitch* is sinking, it won't waste another torpedo, but will surface. He orders his men to set a small fire on the deck to fool the enemy.

Rossi is right, and when the smoke rises from the deck, the U-boat surfaces. Before the sub can crash dive, the *Seawitch* rams it and sends it to the bottom.

The *Seawitch* rejoins the convoy and, beneath a squadron of Russian escort planes, reaches the port of destination, Murmansk.

Directed by Lloyd Bacon. Produced by Jerry Wald. Screenplay by John Howard Lawson. Based on a story by Guy Gilpatrick. Release date, June 1943. A Warner Brothers-First National Picture.

| | |
|---|---|
| Joe Rossi | *Humphrey Bogart* |
| Capt. Steve Jarvis | *Raymond Massey* |
| Boats O'Hara | *Alan Hale* |
| Pearl | *Julie Bishop* |
| Sarah Jarvis | *Ruth Gordon* |
| Chips Abrams | *Sam Levene* |
| Johnnie Pulaski | *Dane Clark* |
| Whitey Lara | *Peter Whitney* |
| Rear Admiral Hartridge | *Minor Watson* |
| Caviar Jinks | *J. M. Kerrigan* |
| Cadet Robert Parker | *Dick Hogan* |
| Ensign Wright | *Kane Richmond* |
| Goldberg | *Chick Chandler* |
| Cecil | *George Offerman, Jr.* |
| Lt. Commander | *Don Douglas* |
| Pete Larson | *Art Foster* |
| Ahearn | *Ray Montgomery* |
| Sparks | *Creighton Hale* |
| Hennessy | *Elliott Sullivan* |
| McGonigle | *Alec Craig* |
| Capt. Ziemer | *Ludwig Stossell* |
| Cherub | *Dick Wessel* |
| Capt. Carpolis | *Frank Puglia* |
| Jenny O'Hara | *Iris Adrian* |

*With Raymond Massey*

123

# Thank Your Lucky Stars

Directed by David Butler. Produced by Mark Hellinger. Screenplay by Norman Panama, Melvin Frank, and James V. Kern. From an original story by Everett Freeman and Arthur Schwartz. Release date, September 1943. A Warner Brothers-First National Picture.

| | |
|---|---|
| Himself | *Humphrey Bogart* |
| Himself and Joe Simpson | *Eddie Cantor* |
| Herself | *Bette Davis* |
| Herself | *Olivia de Havilland* |
| Himself | *Errol Flynn* |
| Himself | *John Garfield* |
| Pat Dixon | *Joan Leslie* |
| Herself | *Ida Lupino* |
| Tom Randolph | *Dennis Morgan* |
| Herself | *Ann Sheridan* |
| Herself | *Dinah Shore* |
| Herself | *Alexis Smith* |
| Himself | *Jack Carson* |
| Himself | *Alan Hale* |
| Himself | *George Tobias* |
| Farnsworth | *Edward Everett Horton* |
| Dr. Schlenna | *S. Z. Sakall* |
| Gossip | *Hattie McDaniel* |
| Nurse Hamilton | *Ruth Donnelly* |
| Announcer | *Don Wilson* |
| Soldier | *Willie Best* |
| Angelo | *Henry Armetta* |
| Girl with a Book | *Joyce Reynolds* |

With: *Spike Jones and His City Slickers.*

Producers Farnsworth and Schlenna are attending the Eddie Cantor radio show, scouting talent for a mammoth Cavalcade of Stars benefit. They want Dinah Shore but not Cantor.

After the show, Barney Jackson, a phony Hollywood agent, slips Cantor a piece of paper to sign. It turns out to be a contract for Tommy Randolph to appear on the Cantor show. Barney collects sixty dollars from Randolph as commission. Barney exits quickly when he meets Pat Dixon, a songwriter, who demands the return of the commission she has paid Barney.

Pat follows him in a "see the movie stars' homes" bus. The driver is Joe Simpson, a slightly shaggy double for Cantor. Joe is an actor who can't get a job because he looks so much like Cantor.

Joe takes Pat to Gower Gulch, where out-of-work actors live, and there she meets Randolph, who is celebrating the fact that he has signed a contract to sing on the Cantor show.

Farnsworth and Schlenna are forced to accept Cantor as the chairman of the entertainment committee. Cantor takes over, disrupting all their plans. Randolph finds out that his contract is a fake, but Pat Dixon has a plan.

A trio of Gower Gulch Indians appear at the theatre and lure Cantor away by saying a young lady from *Life* magazine is waiting to take pictures of them adopting him as an honorary chief. They take him to a Gower Gulch basement. With a haircut, minus his glasses, and looking exactly like Cantor, Joe appears at the theatre. He agrees to stop interfering with the show if Farnsworth and Schlenna will use Tommy Randolph. All agree.

The benefit starts brilliantly, but word comes that Cantor has escaped. Bette Davis, Humphrey Bogart, and Ida Lupino are sensations. Errol Flynn is a riot. Bette Davis bowls over the capacity audience with the "They're Either Too Young Or Too Old" number. But Cantor is on the way.

With the finale still ahead, Pat, Tommy, and Joe wait backstage. Farnsworth rushes to them with a telegram for "Cantor." It's from J. L. Warner, offering Randolph a movie contract.

Tommy and Pat embrace. Cantor bursts backstage, wild-eyed, still in redskin regalia. He is accompanied by police, and is revenge-bent for trouble.

Then Joe, the actor who never had a chance, rises to the occasion. He convinces everybody, including two of Cantor's own stooges, that he is the real Cantor, and the "impostor" is thrown out. The finale goes on triumphantly.

# Sahara

The fall of Tobruk strands the *Lulubelle*, a 28-ton American tank, in a desert full of conquering Nazis. Rather than let his beloved *Lulubelle* fall into unkind hands, her commander, Sgt. Joe Gunn, and his crew point her snub nose in the general direction of the retreating Eighth Army and take their chances in an uncharted wilderness of sandstorms and bone-dry water holes.

By the time *Lulubelle* caterpillars into the deserted caravan station of Bir Acroma, her passenger list has been augmented by three Tommies, stragglers under the command of Captain Jason Halliday; a South African; a British medical officer; a Sudanese corporal and his repentant Italian prisoner. Another prisoner is added when a Messerschmitt that attacks the tank is downed and its arrogant pilot captured.

Shortly after the *Lulubelle's* men find that Bir Acroma's well is a subterranean trickle that can be milked for only a few gallons, they discover that a German column, even more desperately in need of water, is hopefully making its way to the oasis.

The *Lulubelle* and her crew could make a run for it, but instead they vote to delay the enemy as long as possible, first by demanding a wholesale surrender of the Nazi hundreds in exchange for the water that isn't there.

In order to fool the Nazis, Sgt. Gunn, stripped to the waist, splashes luxuriously and ostentatiously in a bucket of imaginary water.

It turns out that the *Lulubelle* and three men live to hear that the British have stood firm at Alamein, and their fighting has not been in vain.

Directed by Zoltan Korda. Screenplay by John Howard Lawson and Zoltan Korda. Adaptation by James O'Hanlon. From a story by Philip MacDonald. Based on an incident in the Soviet photoplay *The Thirteen*. Release date, October 1943. A Columbia Picture.

| | |
|---|---|
| Sgt. Joe Gunn | *Humphrey Bogart* |
| Waco Hoyt | *Bruce Bennett* |
| Fred Clarkson | *Lloyd Bridges* |
| Tambul | *Rex Ingram* |
| Giuseppe | *J. Carroll Naish* |
| Jimmy Doyle | *Dan Duryea* |
| Capt. Jason Halliday | *Richard Nugent* |
| Ozzie Bates | *Patrick O'Moore* |
| Jean Leroux | *Louis Mercier* |
| Marty Williams | *Carl Harbord* |
| Peter Stegman | *Guy Kingsford* |
| Capt. Von Schletow | *Kurt Kreuger* |
| Major Von Falken | *John Wengraf* |
| Sgt. Krause | *Hans Schumm* |

# Passage To Marseille

Directed by Michael Curtiz. Produced by Hal B. Wallis. Screenplay by Casey Robinson and Jack Moffitt. From a novel by Charles Nordhoff and James Norman Hall. Release date, March 1944. A Warner Brothers-First National Picture.

| | |
|---|---|
| Matrac | *Humphrey Bogart* |
| Captain Freycinet | *Claude Rains* |
| Paula | *Michele Morgan* |
| Renault | *Philip Dorn* |
| Major Duval | *Sydney Greenstreet* |
| Marius | *Peter Lorre* |
| Petit | *George Tobias* |
| Garou | *Helmut Dantine* |
| Manning | *John Loder* |
| Captain Malo | *Victor Francen* |
| Grandpère | *Vladimir Sokoloff* |
| Chief Engineer | *Eduardo Ciannelli* |
| Singer | *Corinna Mura* |
| First Mate | *Konstantin Shayne* |
| Lieut. Hastings | *Stephen Richards* |
| Lieut. Lenoir | *Charles La Torre* |
| Jourdain | *Hans Conried* |
| Second Mate | *Monte Blue* |
| Mess Boy | *Billy Roy* |
| Bijou | *Frederick Brunn* |
| Second Engineer | *Louis Mercier* |

At a camouflaged airport on the south coast of England, Manning, an American reporter, is getting the story of a fighting Free-French squadron based there from the liaison officer, Captain Freycinet.

Freycinet's narration goes back to the beginning of the war, on a ship bound for Marseille, carrying six thousand tons of nickel ore. The vessel comes on a boat adrift with five semi-conscious men on board.

The skipper, Captain Malo, takes the men on board. The act of mercy fails to meet with the approval of Major Duval, who hates the Republic and is an admirer of Marshall Pétain.

Renault, one of the men rescued, tells what happened. They are escaped prisoners from Devil's Island. There the men had heard about the war, and they were concerned because they still loved France, even though they were convicts. The men are Renault, a deserter from the French Army; Marius, a pickpocket; Garou, a murderer; Petit, a simple-minded farmer; and Matrac, a French journalist whose opposition to the appeasers at the time of Munich resulted in his conviction on a trumped-up charge of murder and treason. They had escaped in order to help France in its time of trouble in the war.

The ship's routine is normal until the news of France's surrender comes over the wireless. This provokes a crisis. Captain Malo has no intention of continuing to Marseille, where his cargo would fall into the hands of the Nazis. Major Duval wants them to go to Marseille.

Captain Malo orders the ship to go to England, but Major Duval takes over the ship. Matrac and his friends turn the tables on Duval, and they go to England.

This ends Freycinet's story. He concludes by telling what the various people are doing now. Matrac is a member of the crew of a bomber which is returning from a mission over the continent; Garou is a mechanic on the base; Petit is a member of a submarine crew; Renault is a commando; Captain Malo is in command of a mine sweeper; Major Duval and his Fascist underlings are all in an English prison.

As the narrative ends, Matrac's bomber returns. He is dead.

*With
Peter
Lorre,
Helmut
Dantine,
and
George
Tobias*

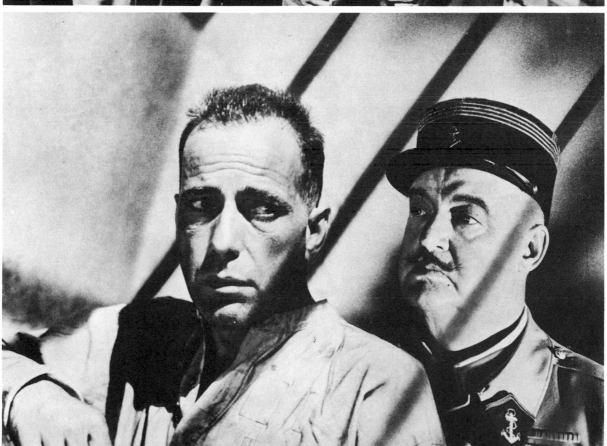

*With
Sydney
Greenstreet*

# Conflict

It is their fifth wedding anniversary, and Richard and Katherine Mason attend a dinner in their honor. They quarrel. She accuses him of an infatuation for her younger sister, Evelyn. Mason does not deny it.

On the way home Mason has an automobile accident. Katherine and Evelyn escape injury, but he suffers a leg wound. He pretends that he cannot walk, and he is confined to a wheel chair. Alone, he walks without trouble.

At the last moment he pleads business and cancels a trip he has planned with Katherine to a mountain resort. He induces her to go alone, promising that he will join her the next day.

Reaching a lonely stretch of mountain road, she finds a car blocking her path. Her husband is there. He kills her and sends her body over a cliff in the car. Then he returns home and tells the police that his wife is missing.

Dr. Hamilton, a psychiatrist friend of the family, is present when Mason tells his story to the police. One thing interests him. Mason describes his wife as wearing a rose when she left home. But Dr. Hamilton gave her the rose when she stopped at his home on the way to the resort. Mason plays his role convincingly, but strange things start to happen.

He walks into the bedroom and smells a familiar perfume—Katherine's perfume. Pieces of jewelry she wore that last day keep appearing. A pawn ticket is found with Katherine's writing on it.

Through all the troubled days he pays court to Evelyn, who is attracted, but draws back out of loyalty to her dead sister.

Finally, when Mason begins to doubt his own sanity, he even sees Katherine, only to lose her in the crowd. To set his doubts at rest he decides upon a drastic step. He will visit the place where the car lies wrecked on the lonely mountainside.

He does, and as he appears, he finds Dr. Hamilton and the police waiting for him. As he marches back to the police cars, his first step to prison, he understands what has happened. The strange incidents were contrived by Dr. Hamilton to lead him to this final trap.

Directed by Curt Bernhardt. Produced by William Jacobs. Screenplay by Arthur T. Horman and Dwight Taylor. Based on an original story by Robert Siodmak and Alfred Neuman. Release date, June 1945. A Warner Brothers Picture.

| | |
|---|---|
| Richard Mason | *Humphrey Bogart* |
| Evelyn Turner | *Alexis Smith* |
| Dr. Mark Hamilton | *Sydney Greenstreet* |
| Katherine Mason | *Rose Hobart* |
| Prof. Norman Holdsworth | *Charles Drake* |
| Dr. Grant | *Grant Mitchell* |
| Det. Lt. Egan | *Patrick O'Moore* |
| Robert Freslon | *Frank Wilcox* |
| Phillips | *Ed Stanley* |
| Det. Lt. Workman | *James Flavin* |
| Landlady | *Mary Servoss* |

# To Have And Have Not

Produced and directed by Howard Hawks. Screenplay by Jules Furthman and William Faulkner. From the novel by Ernest Hemingway. Release date, January 1945. A Warner Brothers-First National Picture.

| | |
|---|---|
| Harry Morgan | *Humphrey Bogart* |
| Eddie (The Rummy) | *Walter Brennan* |
| Marie | *Lauren Bacall* |
| Helene De Bursac | *Dolores Moran* |
| Crickett | *Hoagy Carmichael* |
| Paul De Bursac | *Walter Molnar* |
| Lieut. Coyo | *Sheldon Leonard* |
| Gerard | *Marcel Dalio* |
| Johnson | *Walter Sande* |
| Capt. Renard | *Dan Seymour* |
| Capt. Renard's Bodyguard | *Aldo Nadi* |
| Beauclerc | *Paul Marion* |
| Mrs. Beauclerc | *Patricia Shay* |
| Bartender | *Pat West* |
| Emil | *Emmett Smith* |
| Horatio | *Sir Lancelot* |

Harry Morgan, an American skipper of a cabin cruiser, lives on Martinique after the fall of France. He lives in a hotel with Gerard, the leader of the Free French. Gerard wants Morgan to help the Free French, but the price isn't high enough for the risk involved. Morgan refuses.

That same night, Mr. Johnson, Morgan's employer, is killed, and Morgan finds himself broke. He meets Marie, an American girl just arrived from Trinidad. He vows to help her return to the U.S.

Marie knows that he is broke. She also knows of the Free French offer by which he can make some money. She begs him not to take the assignment. Morgan disregards her warning and gets an advance from Gerard. As he leaves on the mission he leaves a ticket back to the U.S. for Marie.

Morgan is accompanied on the dangerous job by Eddie, an old rummy. Morgan looks after him. Following instructions, Morgan picks up two people from an islet: Paul De Bursac and his wife, Helene. On the way back, they are accosted by a Vichy patrol boat, but they escape after Paul is wounded. When he returns, he finds that Marie has not left.

Morgan becomes more involved when he helps hide the Bursacs from the Vichy police. He finds Captain Renard plying Eddie with liquor to get information, and Renard tells Morgan he can solve all his financial problems by turning over the Bursacs to the police.

Morgan finally decides that he has had enough. He feels that it isn't his war or his problem. He is about to leave when Helene makes an impassioned plea. Morgan is impressed, but he has made up his mind to leave. He goes to find Eddie. But Eddie has disappeared. Captain Renard and two subordinates soon make it clear where Eddie is. They burst into Morgan's room and tell him that the game is up. They have Eddie and will break him by refusing him liquor. It is now Morgan's fight.

Morgan subdues the three men and forces Renard to make a call which frees Eddie. Leaving Renard and his men under Gerard's guard, Morgan goes to get Marie. She's ready. He tells her that it will be a tough road traveling with him, but he wants her. Marie goes with him.

*With Walter Sande and Walter Brennan*

*With Lauren Bacall*

# The Big Sleep

Two-fisted private detective Philip Marlowe is called in by General Sternwood. The General has two daughters, Vivian and Carmen, both beautiful and spoiled. Carmen is being blackmailed by a smut-book dealer named Geiger, and this is the reason Marlowe has been called in. However, Marlowe soon realizes that the chief concern of the General and Vivian is for Shawn Regan. Regan has disappeared, and although he is too proud to admit it, the old man, who loved him like a son, really wants Marlowe to find him.

Marlowe starts to work on the case by investigating Geiger. After hearing shots outside Geiger's home, Marlowe breaks in to find Carmen dressed in Oriental clothes and obviously drugged. At her feet is Geiger—dead. The photos with which Geiger has been blackmailing Carmen are now missing.

Vivian visits Marlowe's office with news that Carmen has received more blackmail demands—from Joe Brody, who has taken over Geiger's business. Marlowe forces Brody to return the photos.

Throughout the investigation Marlowe has come up against Eddie Mars, a big-shot racketeer. Shawn Regan is supposed to have eloped with Mars's wife, Mona. Marlowe determines to find Regan, even though Mars and Vivian want him to drop the investigation.

Proceeding with his investigation, Marlowe falls into the clutches of Eddie's gunmen in their hide-out, where he also finds Mona and Vivian. Vivian helps him make his getaway after a gun duel in which Marlowe has to kill a man. Rushing with her to the Geiger house, Marlowe traps Eddie Mars into meeting him there and covers him. He learns that Mars has murdered the missing Regan and has convinced Vivian that her wild sister, Carmen, was his accomplice. Hence Vivian's efforts to get Marlowe off Regan's trail, to keep her sister from being involved, and to keep her father's heart from being broken before the old man, as Marlowe puts it, goes into the "big sleep."

Outside of Geiger's house, Mars's gunmen are waiting to wipe out Marlowe when he steps out. Instead, he forces Mars himself to go first, and Mars meets his own death, at his own direction. Shaken by their experience together and deciding to send Carmen away for proper care, Marlowe and Vivian send for Bernie Ohls, the D.A.'s man—and the siren of his approaching car plays an accompaniment to their affectionate embrace at the fade-out.

Directed by Howard Hawks. Screenplay by William Faulkner, Leigh Brackett, and Jules Furthman. From the novel by Raymond Chandler. Release date, August 1946. A Howard Hawks Production. A Warner Brothers-First National Picture.

| | |
|---|---|
| Philip Marlowe | *Humphrey Bogart* |
| Vivian | *Lauren Bacall* |
| Eddie Mars | *John Ridgely* |
| Carmen | *Martha Vickers* |
| Proprietress | *Dorothy Malone* |
| Mona Mars | *Peggy Knudsen* |
| Bernie Ohls | *Regis Toomey* |
| General Sternwood | *Charles Waldron* |
| Norris (Butler) | *Charles D. Brown* |
| Canino | *Bob Steele* |
| Harry Jones | *Elisha Cook, Jr.* |
| Joe Brody | *Louis Jean Heydt* |
| Agnes | *Sonia Darrin* |
| Capt. Cronjager | *James Flavin* |
| Wilde | *Thomas Jackson* |
| Carol Lundgren | *Tom Rafferty* |
| Arthur Geiger | *Theodore Von Eltz* |
| Owen Taylor | *Dan Wallace* |
| Taxicab Driver | *Joy Barlowe* |
| Sidney | *Tom Fadden* |
| Pete | *Ben Welden* |
| Art Huck | *Trevor Bardette* |

# The Two Mrs. Carrolls

Directed by Peter Godfrey. Produced by Mark Hellinger. Screenplay by Thomas Job. From the play by Martin Vale. Release date, May 1947. A Warner Brothers-First National Picture.

| | |
|---|---|
| Geoffrey Carroll | *Humphrey Bogart* |
| Sally | *Barbara Stanwyck* |
| Cecily Latham | *Alexis Smith* |
| Dr. Tuttle | *Nigel Bruce* |
| Mrs. Latham | *Isobel Elsom* |
| Charles Pennington | *Patrick O'Moore* |
| Beatrice Carroll | *Ann Carter* |
| Christine | *Anita Bolster* |
| Mr. Blagdon | *Barry Bernard* |
| MacGregor | *Colin Campbell* |
| First Tout | *Peter Godfrey* |
| Second Tout | *Creighton Hale* |

Geoffrey Carroll, an American artist living in England, is in love with Sally Morton. There is only one problem: Carroll is already married. Carroll surreptitiously buys some poison from a chemist named Blagdon, who recognizes Carroll.

One night, after bringing his wife her nightly glass of warm milk, Carroll explains to his daughter that he must send her away to school because of her mother's illness.

Some two years later, the "first Mrs. Carroll" is dead, and Geoffrey has married Sally. Carroll then meets Cecily Latham, and they fall in love.

Sally becomes unaccountably ill, and Geoffrey is kinder than ever to her. Each night he brings her a glass of warm milk. Blagdon starts to blackmail Geoffrey. Blagdon calls him and tells him to come to London. Carroll leaves as Sally is helping his daughter get ready to go back to school.

The child tells Sally that the last time she went to school her mother had died, and also lets slip the fact that Geoffrey had always brought her mother milk before retiring. Sally is convinced that Geoffrey is trying to poison her.

In London, Geoffrey kills Blagdon to end the blackmail and then returns to a planned dinner party. Sally tells Pennington, an ex-suitor and friend of the family, that she has something to tell him.

After the guests leave, Sally confronts Geoffrey with what the child has told her. Geoffrey is evasive, and he goes to get her some warm milk. Sally doesn't have time to get her revolver, but she manages to throw the milk out of the window. She spills some on the sill. Sally pretends to have finished the milk and then goes into her room. Geoffrey carefully washes out the glass, but notices that there is some on the sill. He knows that Sally knows his plan. She must not live.

Sally manages to call Pennington before Geoffrey demands she come out of her room. She refuses to unlock the door. Geoffrey, a wild figure, soaked with rain, climbs up the branch of a tree and pushes open the casement window of Sally's room. Wildly he tells her that he is going to make her drink a small bottle of poison, and then, when she is asleep, he is going to strangle her—blaming a burglar. Sally tries to cover him with her revolver, but he wrests it from her.

Pennington bursts into the house with the police. Geoffrey drinks the poison he has tried to force on Sally and falls dead.

137

# Dead Reckoning

Rip Murdock, a paratroop captain, and Sgt. Johnny Drake, his buddy, are summoned home from abroad to be decorated for their outstanding combat records. While their train rests in Philadelphia, Drake disappears when reporters come to interview him. Rip, aware that his friend has been concealing something in his past and has even enlisted under an assumed name, tries to trace him. He learns Drake's real name through his fraternity key and traces him to a small southern town. There, by diligent probing, Rip discovers that Drake, before his enlistment, was implicated in the murder of the wealthy husband of Coral Chandler, a beautiful blonde, and escaped from the police when picked up for questioning.

Meanwhile, before he can contact Drake, Drake is killed in an auto crash. His charred body is identified by Rip. Drake has been murdered. Not satisfied that his dead friend was the murderer of Coral's husband, Rip visits the night club of a shady character named Martinelli, in order to question Louis Ord, a waiter who was a witness at the Chandler inquest.

Before the waiter can give him a letter intended for Rip by his dead friend, the waiter is murdered and his body placed in Rip's room. Rip disposes of the body. He tries to get the letter from Martinelli's office, but is beaten by a henchman. Rip had smelled Coral's perfume in the room. However, Rip has fallen for her. He escapes and picks up Coral, who confesses that she, not Drake, killed her husband. She pleads self-defense. They go to Martinelli's office to get the revolver that she used as the murder weapon, and they plan to leave town together.

Rip is forced to use incendiary jelly bombs to blast the secret of the gun's hiding place from Martinelli, and they all flee from the burning office. Martinelli, in the lead, is shot down by Coral, who attempts to escape in her car without Rip. He overtakes her, however, and seizes the wheel. He accuses her of really intending to shoot him instead of Martinelli. Coral demands the return of the Chandler murder weapon and shoots Rip when he refuses to give it to her. The car, out of control, crashes. Coral dies of her injuries. Rip survives and is free to clear the name of his dead pal.

Directed by John Cromwell. Screenplay by Oliver H. P. Garrett and Steve Fisher. Adaptation by Allen Rivkin. From a story by Gerald Adams and Sidney Biddell. Release date, February 1947. A Columbia Picture.

| | |
|---|---|
| Rip Murdock | *Humphrey Bogart* |
| Coral Chandler | *Lizabeth Scott* |
| Martinelli | *Morris Carnovsky* |
| Lt. Kincaid | *Charles Cane* |
| Johnny Drake | *William Prince* |
| Krause | *Marvin Miller* |
| McGee | *Wallace Ford* |
| Father Logan | *James Bell* |
| Louis Ord | *George Chandler* |
| Lt. Col. Simpson | *William Forrest* |
| Hyacinth | *Ruby Dandridge* |

# Dark Passage

Directed by Delmar Daves. Produced by Jerry Wald. Screenplay by Delmar Daves. From the novel by David Goodis. Release date, September 1947. A Warner Brothers-First National Picture.

| | |
|---|---|
| Vincent Parry | *Humphrey Bogart* |
| Irene Jansen | *Lauren Bacall* |
| Bob | *Bruce Bennett* |
| Madge Rapf | *Agnes Moorehead* |
| Sam, a Cabby | *Tom D'Andrea* |
| Baker | *Clifton Young* |
| Detective | *Douglas Kennedy* |
| George Fellsinger | *Rory Mallinson* |
| Dr. Walter Coley | *Houseley Stevenson, Jr.* |

Vincent Parry, who has been convicted of the murder of his wife, escapes from San Quentin. Almost as soon as he is out, he is approached by an expensively dressed blonde, Irene Jansen. She helps him get to her apartment in San Francisco.

Irene explains how her interest in him was motivated by the startling similarity between his case and her father's. Wealthy Calvin Jansen had been convicted on circumstantial evidence and died in prison.

Parry is suspicious of Irene because of her association with Bob Rapf and his estranged wife, Madge. Madge is attractive but vicious. It was her claimed eyewitness testimony that convicted him.

Parry visits his close friend George Fellsinger, who agrees to let him use his apartment for a few days. Parry then undergoes plastic surgery to change his face. The operation is a success, but in the meantime George has been murdered.

With his new face and new name, Allan Linnell, Parry is determined to find out who really killed his wife and George.

He escapes from a suspicious detective to a cheap hotel room, and is almost immediately approached by a Mr. Arbogast. Arbogast turns out to be a smalltime crook bent on blackmail. Pretending to agree to a scheme to extort $60,000 from Irene, Parry drives the man to an abandoned quarry. He learns that Madge is the guilty party and later accuses her of the double murder.

To further her own desire for Parry, Madge had killed his wife. But when he spurned her love, she falsely accused him at the trial. Her selfish mind was warped with the obsession that if she couldn't have him, no one would.

After learning that he was hiding in Irene's apartment, she maneuvered to make certain that his escape from prison would end in the death chamber for the murder of his friend George.

Unable to escape the web of evidence in which Parry has enmeshed her, Madge leaps through an apartment window. With his last hope of clearing his name lying dead on the pavement below, Parry decides to leave the country.

From a telephone booth in the waiting room of a shabby bus terminal, he calls Irene and explains what has happened. She understands and promises to meet him in a little town on the coast of Peru.

Parry boards the bus for Mexico, first stop on the way to freedom.

*With Lauren Bacall*

# The Treasure Of The Sierra Madre

Dobbs and Curtin are both Americans on the bum in Tampico, Mexico, in 1920. They are dirty, unshaven, and very much down on their luck. Dobbs wins a lottery, about a hundred dollars. Together with Howard, an oldtime prospector, they decide to go on a gold-hunting trip to the mountains.

Their hard trip begins, marked by surface friendship and small talk among the three. Their train is unsuccessfully ambushed by bandits. The leader of the bandits is distinguished by his gold-colored hat.

Bitterness starts to set in. This is increased when they discover gold and strike it rich. Dobbs must be repeatedly cooled down by the other two, as he falsely accuses them of trying to steal his share. Tension mounts daily, becomes almost unbearable during the long Mexican nights.

Cody, another American, visits their camp and demands a share of the gold, but he is killed when they are all attacked by Gold Hat. The bandits are scattered.

They decide to head back for civilization. The trip becomes a nightmare, due to the fortune each man carries and his general distrust for the others. Again it is Dobbs who is the troublemaker, old man Howard, the soother.

En route down the mountain the three are overtaken by friendly Indians who tell of a dying boy in their camp. Old Howard pulls the boy through, and the Indians make him a virtual prisoner as their own medicine man, leaving Dobbs and Curtin to go it alone.

As was to be expected, the quibbling between the two, brought on solely by Dobbs, leads to gunplay. Giving Curtin up for dead, Dobbs goes on alone, with all the treasure in his possession. His troubles multiply on the trail, and he is finally slain by Gold Hat and his boys, who rip open the saddlebags and unknowingly scatter the gold to the winds.

Curtin revives. Howard and Curtin arrive in an outpost town to hear the whole gruesome story, including Gold Hat's apprehension by the Federales.

Returning to the tribe that adopted him, Howard tells Curtin: "Laugh, Curtin, old boy. It's a great joke played on us by the Lord or fate or by Nature... whichever you prefer, but whoever or whatever played it, certainly has a sense of humor. The gold has gone back to where we got it. Laugh, my boy, laugh. It's worth ten months of labor and suffering... this joke is."

Directed by John Huston. Produced by Henry Blanke. Screenplay by John Huston. Based on the novel by B. Traven. Release date, January 1948. A Warner Brothers-First National Picture.

| | |
|---|---|
| Dobbs | *Humphrey Bogart* |
| Howard | *Walter Huston* |
| Curtin | *Tim Holt* |
| Cody | *Bruce Bennett* |
| McCormick | *Barton MacLane* |
| Gold Hat | *Alfonso Bedoya* |
| Presidente | *A. Soto Rangel* |
| El Jefe | *Manuel Donde* |
| Pablo | *José Torvay* |
| Pancho | *Margarito Luna* |
| Flashy Girl | *Jacqueline Dalya* |
| Mexican Boy | *Bobby Blake* |
| Man in a White Suit | *John Huston* |

# Key Largo

Directed by John Huston. Produced by Jerry Wald. Screenplay by Richard Brooks and John Huston. Based on a play by Maxwell Anderson. Release date, July 1948. A Warner Brothers-First National Picture.

| | |
|---|---|
| Frank M'Cloud | *Humphrey Bogart* |
| Johnny Rocco | *Edward G. Robinson* |
| Nora Temple | *Lauren Bacall* |
| James Temple | *Lionel Barrymore* |
| Gaye | *Claire Trevor* |
| Curly | *Thomas Gomez* |
| Toots | *Harry Lewis* |
| Deputy Clyde Sawyer | *John Rodney* |
| Angel | *Dan Seymour* |
| Ziggy | *Marc Lawrence* |
| Ben Wade | *Monte Blue* |
| Osceola Brother | *Jay Silverheels* |
| Osceola Brother | *Rodric Red Wing* |

Frank M'Cloud, a disillusioned ex-Army major, arrives at the Largo Hotel in Key Largo. As he enters the hotel he encounters an evil collection of faces: Angel, Toots, Curly, Ralph, and Gaye, a blowsy, hard-drinking blonde.

M'Cloud finds Mr. Temple, the owner of the hotel, and his daughter, just as the sheriff and his deputy arrive looking for two escaped Indian convicts. Nora tells M'Cloud that the unsavory crowd, including a Mr. Brown, who comes out only after dark, will be leaving that same night.

Nora and Temple are held prisoner by the "guests," and when Mr. Brown comes into the room, M'Cloud recognizes him as Rocco, a notorious racketeer supposedly deported from the United States.

Rocco makes a phone call to Ziggy in Miami and then starts to make a play for Nora. Because of this he quarrels with Gaye.

Rocco offers M'Cloud a chance to shoot it out with him, but M'Cloud refuses his challenge. Gaye points out that it is better to be a live coward than a dead hero.

Rocco's nerves are taut to the breaking point. The first blast of a tropical hurricane hits the hotel. Rocco abuses Gaye and then attacks M'Cloud for trying to help her. Rocco refuses shelter to the two Indian convicts.

As the storm reaches its peak and quiets, the sheriff discovers the body of his deputy washed up on the shore. Rocco and his men have killed him. The sheriff fires on and kills the Indians, mistakenly believing that they were responsible for his deputy's death. It is then that M'Cloud decides that he must fight again.

Ziggy arrives from Miami, and he and Rocco split a cache of counterfeit money. Then, with the disappearance of his skipper, Rocco forces M'Cloud to pilot the boat that will take his henchmen back to Cuba.

Once on the boat, a gun battle ensues, and M'Cloud manages to kill them.

From his death-loaded boat, M'Cloud calls Nora on the ship-to-shore telephone and tells her what he has done.

Then he steers the boat back to Key Largo.

*With Edward G. Robinson (above),*
*and Claire Trevor and Lauren Bacall (below)*

# Knock On Any Door

A bigtime lawyer who fought his way out of Skid Row, Andrew Morton defends reform-school graduate Nick "Pretty Boy" Romano, accused of killing a cop.

Morton, who had defended Nick's father some years earlier, watched Nick's downhill slide from the time the older Romano died in prison. He saw the boy gang up with other Skid Row youngsters to hold up and rob pedestrians, to steal from neighborhood stores and sell their loot to fences who buy anything with no questions asked.

Nick winds up in reform school, where he is completely brutalized by a penal system which causes the death of his closest friend. Out again, hating cops, Nick meets and falls in love with Emma and tries to go straight. His inability to provide decently for the girl, and, later, for the baby she expects, turns Nick back to gambling and robbery. Nick barely escapes arrest from a robbery in which a policeman is killed. He returns to Emma, only to find her dead, a suicide.

Morton's defense of Nick is so successful that District Attorney Kerman grows desperate in his efforts to smash Nick's alibi. Nick himself takes the stand and withstands Kerman's onslaught of questions to win additional sympathy.

It looks as if Nick will be acquitted.

Kerman dismisses Nick from the witness chair, when he thinks of another matter, almost absently. What, he asks quietly, caused Emma's death? Did Nick's bad treatment cause her to kill herself?

That does it. Nick goes to pieces and shouts that he will tell them anything they want to know. Sure, he killed the policeman —only leave Emma out of it.

Morton visits Nick just before he goes down the last mile to the chair. He tells Nick that the case has served a purpose. Skid Row is being cleaned up.

Directed by Nicholas Ray. Screenplay by Daniel Taradash and John Monks, Jr. From the novel by Willard Motley. Produced by Robert Lord. Release date, April 1949. A Santana-Columbia Picture.

| | |
|---|---|
| Andrew Morton | *Humphrey Bogart* |
| Nick Romano | *John Derek* |
| District Attorney Kerman | *George Macready* |
| Emma | *Allene Roberts* |
| Judge Drake | *Barry Kelley* |
| Adele | *Susan Perry* |
| Vito | *Mickey Knox* |
| Nelly | *Cara Williams* |
| Kid Fingers | *Jimmy Conlin* |
| Jimmy | *Sumner Williams* |
| Squint | *Sid Melton* |
| Juan | *Pepe Hern* |
| Butch | *Dewey Martin* |
| Sunshine | *Robert A. Davis* |

*With John Derek and Susan Perry*

# Tokyo Joe

Directed by Stuart Heisler. Produced by Robert Lord. Screenplay by Cyril Hume and Bertram Millhauser. Adaptation by Walter Doniger. Release date, November 1949. A Santana Production. A Columbia Picture.

| | |
|---|---|
| Joe Barrett | *Humphrey Bogart* |
| Mark Landis | *Alexander Knox* |
| Trina | *Florence Marly* |
| Baron Kimura | *Sessue Hayakawa* |
| Danny | *Jerome Courtland* |
| Idaho | *Gordon Jones* |
| Ito | *Teru Shimada* |
| Kanda | *Hideo Mori* |
| General Ireton | *Charles Meredith* |
| Colonel Dahlgren | *Rhys Williams* |
| Anya | *Lora Lee Michel* |
| Nani-San | *Kyoko Kama* |
| Kamikaze | *Gene Gondo* |
| Major Loomis | *Harold Goodwin* |
| M. P. Captain | *James Cardwell* |
| Truck Driver | *Frank Kumagai* |
| Takenobu | *Tetsu Komai* |
| Hara | *Otto Han* |
| Goro | *Yosan Tsuruta* |

Joe Barrett, Air Corps hero, sadly returns to Tokyo and the life he walked out on in late 1941, believing his White Russian wife, Trina, had died in a Japanese concentration camp. Joe finds his night club, Tokyo Joe's, still being operated by his partner, Ito, who tells him that Trina is still alive and living in Tokyo. She has divorced Joe and is now married to Mark Landis, an American lawyer; there is a little girl, Anya. Joe tells Trina and Landis that he is determined to win Trina back.

Baron Kimura Danshaku, former head of the Japanese secret service, forces Joe to obtain an airline franchise, by threatening to reveal that Trina has broadcast Japanese propaganda during the war. Trina admits that she committed treason to save the life of her baby—and his. Joe gets Landis's help in obtaining his franchise. Kimura has Joe smuggle three wanted war criminals into Japan. Kimura kidnaps Anya to make absolutely certain that they arrive safely and at the specified time. Joe and his co-pilots, Danny and Idaho, pick up the fugitives, who are captured even though they hijack the plane.

With only an hour to recover Anya, Joe finds Ito has committed hara-kiri in penance for betraying his friend Joe. Before he dies, Ito reveals the Baron's hiding place, a bombed-out cellar.

Joe enters the cellar alone, finds Anya, and kills Kimura's servant, Kanda. Joe himself is shot in the back by Kimura before Kimura is also shot. To the last, Joe believes that he will be reunited with Trina and with their daughter.

*With Alexander Knox and Florence Marly*

# Chain Lightning

Nothing good ever happens to Matt Brennan. Once a highly praised and decorated bomber pilot, he is now a failure. Then he meets Leland Willis, a postwar opportunist who is trying to cash in on the airplane company he has acquired, by making a new jet plane for the Air Force.

At a party, Matt re-encounters Jo Holloway, a girl that he knew and loved during the war. Her escort is another old friend, Carl Troxell, who is working with Willis on the jet.

Jo leaves the party with Matt, and their old love is rekindled.

Troxell induces Willis to hire Matt as the test pilot for the new jet, and the first test assignment is a success. But after the flight, Troxell comes to Matt to tell him that the bailing-out device has not been perfected yet. It is a pressurized cabin called a pod, which ejects the pilot and brings him down safely.

Matt visits Willis and talks him into an over-the-Pole flight to get publicity for the YL-3 and a government order for the plane. Willis agrees, because he plans to sell the planes to the government and then, after the pod is perfected, a whole new batch.

The flight is a success, but when Matt returns he learns that Troxell has been killed testing the pod.

Jo accuses Matt of responsibility for Troxell's death. She wants Matt to fly the jet with the new equipment to prove Troxell's theory works. But Matt refuses.

The last routine test flight of the YL-3 is almost finished, and Willis and the Air Force general have ordered Matt to land the plane. They discover that he is flying the jet with the pod and that he intends to test it against everybody's orders.

Then, as the words of Jo and Troxell come back to him, Matt's thumb presses the switch, and the pod catapults from the fuselage, shoots vertically into the sky, and starts falling at a terrific speed as Matt lies unconscious.

He regains consciousness as the parachute snaps loose and the pod sways gently at the end of the steel cables. It starts its history-making descent to the testing grounds.

The pod is a success, and Jo meets Matt on the field. He crushes her to him.

Directed by Stuart Heisler. Produced by Anthony Veiller. Screenplay by Liam O'Brien and Vincent Evans. Suggested by a story by J. Redmond Prior. Release date, February 1950. A Warner Brothers-First National Picture.

| | |
|---|---|
| Matt Brennan | *Humphrey Bogart* |
| Jo Holloway | *Eleanor Parker* |
| Leland Willis | *Raymond Massey* |
| Carl Troxell | *Richard Whorf* |
| Major Hinkle | *James Brown* |
| General Hewitt | *Roy Roberts* |
| Bostwick | *Morris Ankrum* |
| Mrs. Willis | *Fay Baker* |
| Jeb Farley | *Fred Sherman* |

# In A Lonely Place

Directed by Nicholas Ray. Produced by Robert Lord. Screenplay by Andrew Solt. Based on a story by Dorothy B. Hughes. Adaptation by Edmund H. North. Release date, August 1950. A Santana Production. A Columbia Picture.

| | |
|---|---|
| Dixon Steele | *Humphrey Bogart* |
| Laurel Gray | *Gloria Grahame* |
| Brub Nicolai | *Frank Lovejoy* |
| Captain Lochner | *Carl Benton Reid* |
| Mel Lippman | *Art Smith* |
| Sylvia Nicolai | *Jeff Donnell* |
| Mildred Atkinson | *Martha Stewart* |
| Charlie Waterman | *Robert Warwick* |
| Lloyd Barnes | *Morris Ankrum* |
| Ted Barton | *William Ching* |
| Paul | *Steven Geray* |
| Singer | *Hadda Brooks* |
| Frances Randolph | *Alice Talton* |
| Henry Kesler | *Jack Reynolds* |
| Effie | *Ruth Warren* |
| Martha | *Ruth Gillette* |
| Swan | *Guy Beach* |
| Junior | *Lewis Howard* |

Screenwriter Dixon Steele is callous, insulting, and vicious in his dark, ugly moods, but he can be tender and considerate under the influence of love. He has a deep, spontaneous affection for a broken-down old star who is aglow with brandy and Shakespeare.

Steele is under suspicion for murder because he was the last person to have seen murdered hat-check girl Mildred Atkinson alive. Police detective Brub Nicolai, a wartime friend, brings Steele in for questioning by Captain Lochner.

The police won't buy his story that he had dated the girl and taken her to his house simply because she had read a book he had been asked to turn into a screenplay. His reasoning was simple: Why waste time reading a book he might not like if somebody could give him the plot in half the time?

Laurel Gray, Steele's neighbor, is helpful in alibiing him. The writer falls in love with Laurel, despite his well-known violent rages over trifles. Their romance is watched with mixed emotions by Mel Lippman, Steele's agent and friend, and by Sylvia Nicolai, Brub's wife.

Dixon and Laurel decide to get married. As he becomes increasingly aware of the police net closing in on him, Steele's tensions grow. He begins to suspect that Laurel wants to leave him, thinking he is really the killer.

In a rage at the thought of her leaving him, Steele begins to strangle Laurel—when Brub telephones to say that the police have captured Mildred's killer, her fiance.

Steele is cleared of all suspicion, but he has lost Laurel anyway.

# The Enforcer

Assistant D. A. Martin Ferguson, after four years, feels sure that he has an open-and-shut case against Albert Mendoza, head of a gang of killers who sell murder as a commodity to anyone who has the price to pay.

Joseph Rico, Mendoza's lieutenant, is the only living eyewitness to a Mendoza murder, but he is killed in a fall from a window at police headquarters.

Duke Malloy staggers into police headquarters and admits killing Nina Lombardo, even though he loved her. She was a "hit" and Duke had the "contract." When the police look for the body, they find it missing, and Duke commits suicide in his cell.

Babe Lazich is picked up in connection with the case, and he tells about the gang. An assignment is called a "contract," and the victim is called the "hit." He admits that he has stashed Nina Lombardo's body in a nearby swamp.

Ferguson visits Teresa Davis, Nina's roommate, and tells her that Nina has been murdered. The only thing that Teresa knows about Nina is that her real name is Angela Vetto.

It turns out that Angela had been reported missing some time before, just after she was a witness to a brutal murder. Her father thought that she was dead. The murder was never solved, even though Mendoza had been a prime suspect.

In order to get some clues, Ferguson plays back the tape recording of Rico's testimony. He suddenly gets the clue that he needs. Rico refers to Nina as having blue eyes. The dead girl had brown eyes. Ferguson then realizes that Teresa Davis really is Nina, and the real Teresa was the one killed.

Ferguson hurries to Nina's house, but she has left for a walk. The police learn that the hired gunmen are after her also.

Ferguson uses a loud-speaker in a record shop to warn her to get off the streets and call him on the phone.

As Ferguson goes to an office building lobby to get her, he is followed by the gunmen. But when one killer attempts to shoot Nina, Ferguson beats him to the draw.

Ferguson has saved the real Nina Lombardo and knows at last he has the witness that will send Albert Mendoza to the chair.

Directed by Bretaigne Windust. Produced by Milton Sperling. Written by Martin Rackin. Release date, February 1951. A Warner Brothers-United States Pictures Production.

| | |
|---|---|
| Martin Ferguson | *Humphrey Bogart* |
| Big Babe Lazich | *Zero Mostel* |
| Joseph Rico | *Ted De Corsia* |
| Albert Mendoza | *Everett Sloane* |
| Capt. Frank Nelson | *Roy Roberts* |
| Duke Malloy | *Michael Tolan* |
| Sgt. Whitlow | *King Donovan* |
| Herman | *Robert Steele* |
| Teresa Davis | *Pat Joiner* |
| Thomas O'Hara | *Don Beddoe* |
| Tony Vetto | *Tito Vuolo* |
| Vince | *John Kellogg* |
| Zaca | *Jack Lambert* |
| Olga Kirshen | *Adelaide Klein* |
| Nina Lombardo | *Susan Cabot* |
| Louis, the Barber | *Mario Siletti* |

# Sirocco

Directed by Curtis Bernhardt. Produced by Robert Lord. Screenplay by A. J. Bezzerides and Hans Jacoby. Based on the novel *Coup de Grace*, by Joseph Kessel. Release date, July 1951. A Santana-Columbia Picture.

| | |
|---|---|
| Harry Smith | *Humphrey Bogart* |
| Violette | *Marta Toren* |
| Colonel Feroud | *Lee J. Cobb* |
| General LaSalle | *Everett Sloane* |
| Major Leon | *Gerald Mohr* |
| Balukjian | *Zero Mostel* |
| Nasir Aboud | *Nick Dennis* |
| Emir Hassan | *Onslow Stevens* |
| Flophouse Proprietor | *Ludwig Donath* |
| Achmet | *David Bond* |
| Arthur | *Vincent Renna* |
| Omar | *Martin Wilkins* |
| Major Robbinet | *Peter Ortiz* |
| Colonel Corville | *Edward Colmans* |
| Sergeant | *Al Eben* |

In 1925, Emir Hassan is leading local fighting in Damascus against the French occupation troops. Harry Smith, an expatriate American black-marketeer, supplies most of the guns and the ammunition for the French-fighting Syrians—at a profit. Colonel Feroud, head of the French Intelligence, tries to cut down on the gun smuggling.

Smith meets Violette, a sullen, sophisticated tramp from Cairo, Colonel Feroud's mistress. He implies that he can get her out of Damascus. She is fed up with Colonel Feroud as well as Damascus.

Smith is told that his guns are no longer needed, and he also learns that the Colonel has discovered that he is the gunrunner. Smith has been sold out by a scheming Armenian, Balukjian.

Violette begs to go with Smith when he makes arrangements to get out of the country illegally, but soldiers interrupt and arrest Violette. Later, Smith is arrested.

Feroud offers Smith a deal. He will let him go if he will make arrangements for Feroud to meet Emir Hassan. Feroud wants the meeting to try to arrange a truce between the French and Syrians. Smith agrees, and he is given a pass out, as is Violette. But Feroud is captured. General LaSalle, however, asks Smith to help save Feroud, who is now being held prisoner by Hassan for ransom.

Smith acts as the go-between, and Hassan agrees to let Feroud go, but has Smith killed.

*With Marta Toren*

# The African Queen

It is 1914. Rose is the strait-laced sister of a British missionary in West Africa. Charlie Allnut, the irresponsible, gin-drinking Canadian skipper of *The African Queen* riverboat, warns her and her brother Samuel that the Germans have declared war.

After Charlie leaves, German troops arrive, burn the village and the mission church, and herd off the natives. Samuel's mind gives way under the blow, and Rose is left alone with the dying man.

The broken Samuel dies. Charlie returns. He buries Samuel and offers Rose sanctuary on his boat. He proposes to hide out in the backwaters of the river until the war peters out. That seems like a good idea, since the boat is well stocked with gin and other supplies.

Rose has other ideas. She has courage and a desire to help her country. Learning that Charlie's boat also has blasting gelatin and oxygen cylinders, she goads Charlie into accepting her fantastic scheme. She plans to blow up a German gunboat on a lake miles down the almost unnavigable river.

After a night of tropical rain, Charlie tries to dissuade Rose, but her will is much too strong. With Charlie at the engine and Rose at the tiller, they guide the *Queen* down the rapids; they mend the broken propeller; they survive attacks of insects and leeches; and finally they get past a German fort.

Jubilant at their partial victory, Charlie and Rose embrace and realize that they are in love. Charlie catches Rose's enthusiasm and throws himself into the project with heart and soul. They plan the next stage of the adventure, but there are more dangers ahead than they can imagine. Lost in the delta of the river, Charlie and Rose believe themselves doomed.

But fate takes a hand, and although captured by the Germans, they do destroy the gunboat, though not according to plan.

Directed by John Huston. Produced by S. P. Eagle. Adapted for the screen by James Agee and John Huston from the novel *The African Queen*, by C. S. Forester. Release date, March 1952. A Horizon-Romulus Production released by United Artists.

| | |
|---|---|
| Charlie Allnut | *Humphrey Bogart* |
| Rose Sayer | *Katharine Hepburn* |
| Rev. Samuel Sayer | *Robert Morley* |
| Captain of the *Louisa* | *Peter Bull* |
| First Officer of the *Louisa* | *Theodore Bikel* |
| German Army Officer | *Peter Swanick* |

# Deadline—U.S.A.

Written and directed by Richard Brooks. Produced by Sol C. Siegel. Release date, May 1952. A 20th Century-Fox Picture.

| | |
|---|---|
| Ed Hutcheson | *Humphrey Bogart* |
| Mrs. Garrison | *Ethel Barrymore* |
| Nora | *Kim Hunter* |
| Frank Allen | *Ed Begley* |
| Burrows | *Warren Stevens* |
| Thompson | *Paul Stewart* |
| Rienzi | *Martin Gabel* |
| Schmidt | *Joseph De Santis* |
| Kitty Garrison Geary | *Joyce MacKenzie* |
| Mrs. Willebrandt | *Audrey Christie* |
| Alice Garrison Courtney | *Fay Baker* |
| Cleary | *Jim Backus* |
| Crane | *Carleton Young* |
| Williams | *Selmer Jackson* |
| Judge | *Fay Roope* |
| Headwaiter | *Parley Baer* |
| Telephone Operator | *Bette Francine* |
| City News Editor | *John Doucette* |
| Bentley | *June Eisner* |
| Copy Boy | *Richard Monohan* |
| Headline Writer | *Harry Tyler* |
| Whitey | *Joe Sawyer* |
| Barndollar | *Florence Shirley* |
| Mrs. Schmidt | *Kasia Orzazewski* |
| Mr. White | *Raymond Greenleaf* |
| Attorney Prentiss | *Alex Gerry* |
| Mrs. Burrows | *Irene Vernon* |
| Doctor | *Everett Glass* |
| Watchman | *Tudor Owen* |
| Mr. Greene | *William Forrest* |
| Mr. Blake | *Edward Keane* |
| Captain Finlay | *Clancy Cooper* |
| Wharton | *Tom Powers* |
| Fenway | *Thomas Browne Henry* |
| Lefty | *Ashley Cowan* |
| Police Sergeant | *Howard Negley* |
| Lewis Schaefer | *Phil Terry* |
| Lugerman | *Joe Mell* |
| National Editor | *Luther Crockett* |
| Sally | *Ann McCrea* |
| Henry | *Willis B. Bouchey* |
| Mac | *Paul Dubov* |
| Al Murray | *Harris Brown* |
| City Editor | *Joseph Crehan* |
| Lawyer Hansen | *Larry Dobkin* |

Ed Hutcheson, managing editor of *The Day*, a progressive, independent newspaper, is informed by the paper's owners, Mrs. John Garrison and her two daughters, that the paper is to be sold to *The Standard*. Mrs. Garrison is reluctant to sell, but her daughters comprise the majority vote. Ed protests the sale as the death of *The Day*, but his pleas go unheeded. He decides, however, to publish as usual until the sale is approved by the court in two days.

Disheartened, Ed seeks comfort in his former wife, Nora, whom he still loves. Although she still cares for him, Nora feels that Ed can only be married to a newspaper.

The next morning, reporter George Burrows is found near death, the victim of a beating by thugs in the employ of Tomas Rienzi, the underworld boss. Burrows had been working on a story which would prove that Rienzi controlled all criminal activities in the city.

Furious, Ed orders his staff to throw the book at Rienzi with news stories, editorials, photos, and cartoons. A break develops when events tie Rienzi with the unsolved murder of show girl Sally. One of Ed's reporters discovers that the dead girl had a brother named Herman Schmidt, an underworld hoodlum. Intense probing forces Schmidt to confess that he saw Rienzi's men kill Sally because she refused to return $200,000 which the crime boss had given her for safekeeping. But as Schmidt is about to sign a statement, he is killed by Rienzi's men.

Sally's mother, however, shows up with the $200,000 and a diary implicating Rienzi on every page. Rienzi warns Ed not to print the contents and threatens him with death, but the editor tells the gang lord that he'll see him in jail.

The court, meanwhile, approves the sale of the paper despite Ed's last-ditch plea. Nora realizes now that Ed is quite the man after all, and together they face the future.

*With Ed Begley*

Lt. Ruth McCara, just arrived at Mobile Army Surgical Hospital 66, behind the Korean battle lines, risks her life to save some litter cases when shells start raining, and is reprimanded by Major Jed Webbe. Later, when the hospital is on the move, he tests his tried-and-true wiles on Ruth, but to no avail. At the new hospital base he performs a miraculous operation on a little Korean boy and, when Ruth compliments him, takes advantage of her mood to kiss her. She tells him that she liked the kiss—liked it too much, in fact—but that she's the marrying kind.

Their next encounter is during a rainstorm, when Jed accidentally stumbles into the tent where Ruth is. The tent collapses, deluging them both, and Ruth, realizing that she loves Jed, agrees to a date.

Another nurse, Lt. Laurence, warns Ruth that Jed, who refuses to talk about himself, is probably married. Ruth questions him, but he refuses to tell her about his private life, and when she insists, abruptly leaves her. The following day Captain John Rustford, the helicopter pilot, gives Jed a bottle of Scotch, and he gets drunk and is reprimanded by his superior officer. Ruth, believing that she is to blame, asks for a transfer. Lt. Col. Whalters suggests that she try advancing instead of retreating with Jed if she really wants to help him. Jed responds by admitting that he is divorced and not interested in another marriage.

In surgery, Ruth gets a grenade away from a berserk Korean prisoner and later collapses from nervous exhaustion. Jed comforts her, and she acknowledges her love for him. The next day the unit is forced to evacuate hurriedly, and they are separated. When they meet again at the new base, both know they belong to each other.

Directed by Richard Brooks. Produced by Pandro S. Berman. Screenplay by Richard Brooks. Based on a story by Allen Rivkin and Laura Kerr. Release date, March 1953. A Metro-Goldwyn-Mayer Picture.

| | |
|---|---|
| Major Jed Webbe | *Humphrey Bogart* |
| Lt. Ruth McCara | *June Allyson* |
| Sgt. Orvil Statt | *Keenan Wynn* |
| Lt. Col. Whalters | *Robert Keith* |
| Capt. John Rustford | *William Campbell* |
| Lt. Rose Ashland | *Patricia Tiernan* |
| Lt. Jane Franklin | *Adele Longmire* |
| Lt. Edith Edwards | *Ann Morrison* |
| Adjutant | *Jonathan Cott* |
| Lt. Laurence | *Perry Sheehan* |

*With June Allyson*

# Beat The Devil

Directed by John Huston. Screenplay by John Huston and Truman Capote. Based on the novel by James Helvick. Release date, March 1954. A Santana-Romulus Production, released through United Artists.

| | |
|---|---|
| Billy Dannreuther | *Humphrey Bogart* |
| Gwendolyn Chelm | *Jennifer Jones* |
| Peterson | *Robert Morley* |
| Maria Dannreuther | *Gina Lollobrigida* |
| O'Hara | *Peter Lorre* |
| Harry Chelm | *Edward Underdown* |
| Major Ross | *Ivor Bernard* |
| Ravello | *Marco Tulli* |
| C.I.D. Inspector | *Bernard Lee* |

Billy Dannreuther and his wife, Maria, are waiting in a seaport town on the Mediterranean while repairs are made to an oil pump of the steamer *Nyanga*, by which they are to travel to Africa.

Their fellow passengers will be Harry Chelm and his wife, Gwendolyn, Peterson, Ravello, O'Hara, and Major Jack Ross. The latter four are Dannreuther's "business associates," led by Peterson.

They are out to buy land in Africa containing uranium deposits, but through the use of fraud. Upon learning of the death of a colonial official in Britain, Billy realizes the murder is the work of his associates and is on his guard.

After a series of adventures aboard the *Nyanga*, when she once again resumes her journey, the ship is wrecked by an explosion, and the group, with the exception of Chelm, is beached on a deserted shore where they are picked up by Arabs.

Peterson buys their freedom from the Arabs, only to find a Scotland Yard detective waiting for them regarding the official's murder. They have just about succeeded in lulling his suspicions when Gwendolyn tells the detective about them, and they are arrested.

Dannreuther leaves with Maria and Gwendolyn to join the latter's husband, who has acquired the land containing the uranium deposits.

# The Caine Mutiny

Midshipman Willie Keith, a young Princetonian; Lt. Tom Keefer, a novelist-intellectual; and Lt. Steve Maryk are shipmates aboard the destroyer-minesweeper *Caine* during the early days of World War II. They are serving under a new captain, Lt. Commander Queeg.

While the *Caine* is engaged in target-towing, Queeg spots a sailor with his shirttail out and bawls him out. Helmsman Still-well tries to tell Queeg that the *Caine* is going to turn and cut the towline, but Queeg refuses to listen. The towline is cut, and Queeg refuses to admit that the ship cut the line. He says that the line was defective.

The ship is ordered to join a task force headed for Kwajalein, where their first job is to lead some Marines to a landing. Queeg wants to get in and out as fast as possible, and he leaves some of the landing craft stranded.

Willie feels that Queeg has turned yellow in action, and Keefer is strongly of the opinion that Queeg is suffering from acute paranoia. Maryk won't listen to this talk and threatens to report it to the captain. This is the start of a constant campaign by Keefer to convince his fellow officers that Queeg is insane. Maryk secretly starts a medical log on the captain.

A series of incidents follow, pointing up Queeg's mental un-balance. Maryk comes around to admitting to Keefer that there may be truth to his estimate of Queeg.

During a furious typhoon, Maryk does not agree with the way Queeg is handling the ship. With the *Caine* in danger of foundering, Maryk invokes Navy Article 184, which allows the executive officer to relieve the commanding officer of duty under emergency conditions. Willie backs him up, and Queeg threatens that they will hang for conspiracy to mutiny.

Once brought back to San Francisco, Willie and Maryk are brought before the court-martial. The trial takes place, and it looks as though conviction is certain, for it is pointed out that Queeg has had many good years of experience, while Willie and Maryk lack experience and judgment. But Lt. Barney Greenwald, the defense attorney, through brilliant questioning, brings out the fact that Queeg is unbalanced. Queeg collapses into a helpless, babbling wreck. The astonished court-martial board brings in a verdict of acquittal.

During a victory celebration, Greenwald tells them what he thinks of them: Queeg, an officer with an honorable record, had always defended the country, while the rest were living their sheltered lives.

Directed by Edward Dmytryk. Produced by Stanley Kramer. Screenplay by Stanley Roberts. From the novel by Herman Wouk. Release date, September 1954. A Columbia Picture.

| | |
|---|---|
| Captain Queeg | *Humphrey Bogart* |
| Lt. Barney Greenwald | *José Ferrer* |
| Lt. Steve Maryk | *Van Johnson* |
| Lt. Tom Keefer | *Fred MacMurray* |
| Ensign Willie Keith | *Robert Francis* |
| May Wynn | *May Wynn* |
| Capt. DeVriess | *Tom Tully* |
| Lt. Commander Challee | *E. G. Marshall* |
| Lt. Paynter | *Arthur Franz* |
| Meatball | *Lee Marvin* |
| Capt. Blakely | *Warner Anderson* |
| Horrible | *Claude Akins* |
| Mrs. Keith | *Katharine Warren* |
| Ensign Harding | *Jerry Paris* |

# Sabrina

Produced and directed by Billy Wilder. Written for the screen by Billy Wilder, Samuel Taylor, and Ernest Lehman. From the play, *Sabrina Fair*, by Samuel Taylor. Release date, October 1954. A Paramount Picture.

| | |
|---|---|
| Linus Larrabee | *Humphrey Bogart* |
| Sabrina Fairchild | *Audrey Hepburn* |
| David Larrabee | *William Holden* |
| Oliver Larrabee | *Walter Hampden* |
| Thomas Fairchild | *John Williams* |
| Elizabeth Tyson | *Martha Hyer* |
| Gretchen Van Horn | *Joan Vohs* |
| Baron | *Marcel Dalio* |
| The Professor | *Marcel Hillaire* |
| Maude Larrabee | *Nella Walker* |
| Mr. Tyson | *Francis X. Bushman* |
| Miss McCardle | *Ellen Corby* |
| Margarete (cook) | *Marjorie Bennett* |
| Charles (butler) | *Emory Parnell* |
| Jenny (maid) | *Nancy Kulp* |

Linus and David Larrabee are brothers, and heirs to the huge fortune of their father. Above the garage, on the vast Long Island estate of the Larrabees, lives their chauffeur, Thomas Fairchild, and his young daughter, Sabrina. Sabrina has a hopeless crush on David, the younger brother, but David's only interests are fast cars and the girls of his own social set.

Because David doesn't notice her, Sabrina attempts suicide. She is saved by Linus.

To remove her from the Larrabee influence and also so that she may become a fine cook, Fairchild sends his daughter to Paris. There Sabrina meets an ultrasophisticated, middle-aged baron, who kindly takes it upon himself to transform the plain-looking Sabrina into a woman of culture and fashion.

In the meantime, back in Long Island, Linus, the business genius of the family, seeks to increase the Larrabee fortune through a marriage between David and wealthy Elizabeth Tyson.

Sabrina returns to Long Island, and even though his engagement to Elizabeth has already been announced, David falls in love with the now radiantly beautiful Sabrina.

To make sure that David marries Elizabeth, Linus sets out to keep his brother and the chauffeur's daughter from seeing each other. He reminds Sabrina of her station in life and advises her not to see David any more. But while he is attempting to work out the situation, something happens to Linus. Sabrina's magic goes to work.

Believing he has himself in hand, he hatches a scheme to feign romantic interest in Sabrina himself. He dupes her into getting on the Europe-bound *Liberté* alone. However, his plans go awry when David opens Linus's eyes to the fact that it is he, Linus, who is truly in love with Sabrina.

Then Linus works fast. He hires a tug and catches up with the *Liberté*, while David, amused by the whole thing, decides to marry Elizabeth Tyson.

# The Barefoot Contessa

In an ancient cemetery, Harry Dawes is one of hundreds attending the funeral of a famous movie star, Contessa Torlato-Favrini, born Maria Vargas. He stares at her marble statue and tells the story of her meteoric career.

Harry, a washed-up movie director, is hired by Kirk Edwards, a rich film novice, to write and direct a film about a glamorous woman.

During a talent-hunting trip to Europe, Harry, Kirk, press agent Oscar Muldoon, and Myrna find Maria Vargas singing in a cabaret. They want her for the film.

With a new name, Maria D'Amata, she becomes a star overnight. Her first film, *Black Dawn*, is a sensation, and her next two films are bigger and better. Harry and Maria make the grade together.

At a party Kirk is giving for South American multi-millionaire playboy Alberto Bravano, Bravano makes a play for Maria, even though he believes she belongs to Kirk. They fight, and Maria decides to accept Bravano's offer of a trip on his yacht. Bravano soon discovers that Maria is untouchable, but he enjoys the idea that people believe that she belongs to him. But she meets and falls in love with Count Vincenzo Torlato-Favrini. They marry.

Some months later Maria comes to Harry. She is distraught. She tells Harry that Vincenzo had been mutilated during the war and cannot consummate the marriage. But she tells Harry that she can make Vincenzo happy. She is going to have a child to perpetuate the Torlato-Favrini name.

As she leaves, Harry watches her through the window and sees that she is being followed by Vincenzo. Harry follows them to their palazzo. He rushes inside and hears two shots.

From the shadows, Vincenzo appears, carrying the limp body of Maria. He tells Harry that Maria is dead and so is the other man. They go into the house, and Vincenzo calmly calls the police.

Back at the cemetery, the services are over, and two officers take Vincenzo away. Slowly Harry and his assistant walk away from the statue of Maria Vargas, the last Contessa Torlato-Favrini.

Written and directed by Joseph L. Mankiewicz. Release date, October 1954. A Figaro Production. Released through United Artists.

| | |
|---|---|
| Harry Dawes | *Humphrey Bogart* |
| Maria Vargas | *Ava Gardner* |
| Oscar Muldoon | *Edmond O'Brien* |
| Alberto Bravano | *Marius Goring* |
| Eleanora Torlato-Favrini | *Valentina Cortesa* |
| Vincenzo Torlato-Favrini | *Rossano Brazzi* |
| Jerry | *Elizabeth Sellars* |
| Kirk Edwards | *Warren Stevens* |
| Pedro | *Franco Interlenghi* |
| Myrna | *Mari Aldon* |
| Night Club Proprietor | *Alberto Rabagliati* |
| Busboy | *Enzo Staiola* |
| Maria's Mother | *Maria Zanoli* |
| Maria's Father | *Renato Chiantoni* |
| J. Montague Brown | *Bill Fraser* |
| Mr. Black | *John Parrish* |
| Mr. Blue | *Jim Gerald* |
| The Pretender | *Tonio Selwart* |
| The Pretender's Wife | *Margaret Anderson* |
| Lulu McGee | *Gertrude Flynn* |
| Hector Eubanks | *John Horne* |
| Mrs. Eubanks | *Bessie Love* |
| Drunken Blonde | *Diana Decker* |
| Gypsy Dancer | *Riccardo Rioli* |
| Eddie Blake | *Robert Christopher* |
| Chambermaid | *Anna Maria Paduan* |
| Chauffeur | *Carlo Dale* |

# We're No Angels

Directed by Michael Curtiz. Produced by Pat Duggan. Screenplay by Ranald MacDougall. Based on a play by Albert Husson. Release date, July 1955. A Paramount Picture.

| | |
|---|---|
| Joseph | *Humphrey Bogart* |
| Albert | *Aldo Ray* |
| Jules | *Peter Ustinov* |
| Amelie Ducotel | *Joan Bennett* |
| Felix Ducotel | *Leo G. Carroll* |
| Isabelle Ducotel | *Gloria Talbot* |
| André Trochard | *Basil Rathbone* |
| Paul Trochard | *John Baer* |
| Madame Parole | *Lea Penman* |
| Arnaud | *John Smith* |

Three convicts—Joseph, Albert, and Jules—escape from Devil's Island on Christmas Eve. Albert carries his pet, a poisonous snake called Adolphe, in a basket.

Seeking a hide-out until they can beg, borrow, or counterfeit passports, the convicts take refuge in the home of Felix Ducotel, a benevolent but ineffectual merchant who manages a store for his penny-pinching, ruthless cousin, André Trouchard. Felix isn't as much concerned about the presence of the trio as he is about the coming visit of his cousin, who is sure to fire him when he sees that the shop is losing money.

Though the convicts had planned to rob and perhaps even murder Ducotel, his wife, and their daughter, Isabelle, they weaken under the family's kind treatment, particularly when they are invited to Christmas dinner.

André and his nephew Paul, with whom Isabelle imagines herself in love, arrive. André's arrogant behavior toward the Ducotels so angers the convicts that when the family retires, they hold council to determine what to do with him.

After André examines the books, he is livid with rage, certain that the Ducotels have stolen from him. He's sure Albert's basket contains something belonging to him, so he takes it with him to his room. Since André is determined to handle his own affairs, the convicts permit him to do so. And that's the end of Cousin André.

Paul gleefully claims his uncle's estate, concealing the fact that there's a will (written by the three convicts) leaving half the property to Ducotel.

Paul is a chip off the old block and believes that he is too good for Isabelle. So, when he reports that he has been bitten by a small snake, the convicts bow to the fates.

Now they turn their attention to finding a new romance for the heartbroken Isabelle. Fate lends a hand in the person of a handsome young medical officer.

Much to their amazement, the Ducotels inherit André's fortune. The convicts, dressed in the best clothes of the deceased, start to leave Devil's Island, but change their minds and return to prison, where they believe there are fewer criminals than in the outside world.

*With
Joan
Bennett*

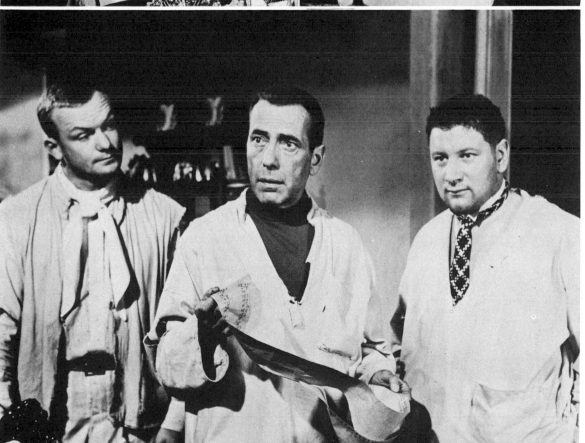

*With
Aldo
Ray
and
Peter
Ustinov*

174

# The Desperate Hours

News of a prison break is received with interest by Dan Hilliard, a typical American business executive living in the suburbs. He returns from work with his daughter Cindy that night and finds his house taken over by the three escaped convicts: Glenn Griffin, sadistic and revenge-ridden killer; Hal, Glenn's younger brother; and Kobish, a ruthless killer.

Sheriff Jesse Bard, the man responsible for Griffin's imprisonment, is the target of the convict's revenge. But before he can kill Bard, Griffin hides out until money reaches him to insure his getaway.

Glenn, the master mind of the trio, tells the family to "make it normal" until the money arrives. Griffin warns Hilliard and his family not to try to get in touch with the police, and threatens to kill them all if they do. A crisis develops when Hilliard's young son, Ralphie, returns from school, discovers the situation, and refuses to let anybody push him around.

Dan finally manages to calm Ralphie and control the tense situation, but another dangerous problem arises when Cindy's boy friend becomes suspicious and tries to enter the house.

For forty-eight terrible hours the pressure on the family mounts. The tension begins to tell on Glenn. First, the money doesn't arrive on schedule. Then, his kid brother, Hal, deserts him.

Glenn finds himself trapped inside the house of the Hilliard family. A clue finally leads the police directly to the house, but with Kobish's gun at the backs of the family, they are helpless to intervene.

Griffin gets word that the money has arrived and he sends Mr. Hilliard to pick it up. The family remains in hostage. Hilliard meets the police and he persuades them to let him return to the house. He takes a revolver with him, an unloaded revolver, for he has a plan.

As soon as Hilliard gets back into the house, Griffin takes the revolver from Hilliard. Naturally he thinks it is loaded. Hilliard provokes a fight between Griffin and Kobish, and Griffin is doomed when the police close in and he pulls the trigger again and again, to no avail.

Hilliard has saved the family.

Produced and directed by William Wyler. Screenplay by Joseph Hayes. Adapted from the novel and play by Joseph Hayes. Release date, November 1955. A Paramount Picture.

| | |
|---|---|
| Glenn Griffin | *Humphrey Bogart* |
| Dan Hilliard | *Fredric March* |
| Jesse Bard | *Arthur Kennedy* |
| Eleanor Hilliard | *Martha Scott* |
| Hal Griffin | *Dewey Martin* |
| Chuck | *Gig Young* |
| Cindy | *Mary Murphy* |
| Ralphie | *Richard Eyer* |
| Kobish | *Robert Middleton* |
| Detective | *Alan Reed* |
| Winston | *Bert Freed* |
| Masters | *Ray Collins* |
| Carson | *Whit Bissell* |
| Fredricks | *Ray Teal* |

# The Left Hand Of God

Directed by Edward Dmytryk. Screenplay by Alfred Hayes. Based on the novel by William E. Barrett. Release date, September 1955. A 20th Century-Fox Production.

| | |
|---|---|
| Jim Carmody | *Humphrey Bogart* |
| Ann Scott | *Gene Tierney* |
| Mieh Yang | *Lee J. Cobb* |
| Beryl Sigman | *Agnes Moorehead* |
| Dr. Sigman | *E. G. Marshall* |
| Mary Yin | *Jean Porter* |
| Rev. Cornelius | *Carl Benton Reid* |
| John Wong | *Victor Sen Yung* |
| Jan Teng | *Philip Ahn* |
| Chun Tien | *Benson Fong* |
| Father O'Shea | *Richard Cutting* |
| Pao-Ching | *Leon Lentok* |
| Father Keller | *Don Forbes* |
| Woman in Sarong | *Noel Toy* |
| Feng-Merchant | *Peter Chong* |
| Woman in Kimona | *Marie Tsien* |
| The Boy | *Stephen Wong* |
| Celeste | *Sophie Chin* |
| Li Kwan | *George Chan* |
| Hospital Orderly | *Walter Soo Hoo* |
| Orderly | *Henry S. Quan* |
| Nurse | *Doris Chung* |
| Old Man | *Moy Ming* |
| Mi Lu | *George Lee* |
| Father | *Beal Wong* |
| Pao Chu | *Stella Lynn* |
| Rev. Marvin | *Robert Burton* |
| Midwife | *Soo Yong* |

The time is 1947 and the place a remote province in China. Jim Carmody is an American flyer who has crashed there and cast his lot with a Chinese warlord, Yang. For three years he has enjoyed the favors of an exotic Eurasian girl, Mary Yin, while captaining the warlord's army, but he wants to return home.

When one of Yang's men kills a priest en route to a mission, Carmody makes his decision. To escape from Yang, who has threatened deserters with death, Carmody disguises himself as a priest and makes his way to the mission.

There he mets Dr. Sigman, his wife, Beryl, and a mission nurse, Ann Scott. Trapped by his masquerade into performing priestly functions, Carmody plans ways of continuing his escape without jeopardizing his new friends. As if the problems posed by the disguise were not enough, Carmody falls in love with Ann. She finds herself strangely attracted to Carmody, but his clerical collar makes her ashamed of this feeling.

At first antagonistic to Carmody, Dr. Sigman and his wife learn to respect the bogus priest when he proves a powerful influence for good in the neglected village. However, Carmody plans to drop his masquerade, and he writes the bishop that he is an imposter.

When Yang, the warlord, catches up with Carmody and threatens to destroy the village and the mission, Carmody makes him an offer. He will gamble five years of loyal service against his freedom and the freedom of the village. They shoot dice, and when Carmody wins, the warlord withdraws.

The bishop's representatives arrive to punish Carmody for his sacrilege, but when they learn of his bravery against the warlord, they promise to intercede in his behalf. Carmody leaves for the coast and whatever penance may be imposed upon him. Ann, now that she knows his true identity, will follow and make known her love when the masquerade is over.

Unemployed sportswriter Eddie Willis reluctantly joins fight racketeer Nick Benko in touting a seven-foot giant from Argentina, Toro Moreno, who can neither punch nor take a punch. In fact, he can't fight at all.

Through fixed fights and circus ballyhoo, Eddie builds Toro into a title contender, with ex-pug George as trainer.

Just before the title fight with champion Buddy Brannen, Toro comes to believe that he has killed an opponent. He refuses to fight again.

Sickened by the mess in which he is involved, Willis nevertheless talks Toro into the title fight. He is brutally beaten in the fight.

Willis gets his pay-off from Benko. He learns that Benko's books show Toro's share of the million-dollar gate is only $49.00, and angrily turns over to the battered giant his own fight money.

Eddie puts Toro aboard a plane for home before Benko can again sell him down the river. At the urging of his wife, Beth, and at the risk of his life, Willis writes a flaming exposé of the dirty fight racket.

Directed by Mark Robson. Produced by Philip Yordan. Screenplay by Philip Yordan. Based on the novel by Budd Schulberg. Release date, April 1956. A Columbia Picture.

| | |
|---|---|
| Eddie Willis | *Humphrey Bogart* |
| Nick Benko | *Rod Steiger* |
| Beth Willis | *Jan Sterling* |
| Toro Moreno | *Mike Lane* |
| Buddy Brannen | *Max Baer* |
| George | *Jersey Joe Walcott* |
| Jim Weyerhause | *Edward Andrews* |
| Art Leavitt | *Harold J. Stone* |
| Luis Agrandi | *Carlos Montalban* |
| Leo | *Nehemiah Persoff* |
| Vince Fawcett | *Felice Orlandi* |
| Max | *Herbie Faye* |
| Danny McKeogh | *Rusty Lane* |
| Tex | *Jack Albertson* |
| Frank | *Val Avery* |
| Tommy | *Tommy Herman* |
| Joey | *Vinnie De Carlo* |
| Gus Dundee | *Pat Comisky* |
| Sailor Rigazzo | *Matt Murphy* |
| Chief Firebird | *Abel Fernandez* |
| Alice | *Marion Carr* |

179

# INDEX

Abel, Walter, 83
"Ace," 46, 47
*Across The Pacific*, 19, 118, 119
*Action In The North Atlantic*, 22, 122, 123
Acuff, Eddie, 51, 63
Adams, Ernie, 64
Adams, Gerald, 139
"Adkins," 44, 45
Adrian, Iris, 123
*African Queen, The*, 24, 25, 158, 159
Agee, James, 159
Ahn, Philip, 176
Akins, Claude, 167
Albert, Eddie, 111
Albertson, Jack, 179
Alcaniz, Luana, 31
Aldon, Mari, 171
Alexander, John, 51
Alexander, Ross, 56
Alison, Joan, 120
Allister, Claude, 76
*All Through The Night*, 19, 114, 115
Allwyn, Astrid, 43
Allyson, June, 162, 163
Alper, Murray, 112, 116
*Amazing Dr. Clitterhouse, The*, 18, 80, 81
Ames, Bobby, 15
Ames, Jean, 115
Anderson, Judith, 115
Anderson, Margaret, 171
Anderson, Maxwell, 144
Anderson, Warner, 167
"Andrew Morton," 23, 146, 147
Andrews, Edward, 179
Andrews, Robert, 59
*Angels With Dirty Faces*, 18, 84, 85
Ankrum, Morris, 151, 152
Armetta, Henry, 124
Astor, Mary, 112, 113, 119
Averill, Anthony, 83
Avery, Val, 179
Aylesworth, Arthur, 67, 87, 92, 95

"Baby Face Martin," 13, 70, 71
Bacall, Lauren, 11, 12, 21, 22, 24, 132, 133, 134, 135, 140, 141, 144, 145
Backus, Jim, 160
Bacon, Irving, 80, 92
Bacon, Lloyd, 64, 67, 83, 92, 99, 104, 123
*Bad Sister*, 15, 36, 37
Baer, John, 172

Baer, Max, 179
Baer, Parley, 160
Baker, Fay, 151, 160
Baker, Graham, 72
Baker, Tommy, 104
Baldwin, Earl, 104
Baldwin, Faith, 76
Bancroft, George, 84
Bardette, Trevor, 92, 135
*Barefoot Contessa, The*, 26, 170, 171
Barlowe, Joy, 135
Barnes, T. Roy, 39
Barrat, Robert, 63
Barrett, William E., 176
Barrie, Mona, 76
Barrie, Wendy, 71
Barrymore, Ethel, 160
Barrymore, Lionel, 144
Bates, Granville, 48, 104
*Battle Circus*, 25, 162, 163
Bazin, André, 11
Beach, Guy, 152
*Beat The Devil*, 25, 164, 165
Beaumont, Gerald, 60
Beavers, Louise, 55
Beddoe, Don, 155
Bedoya, Alfonso, 143
Begley, Ed, 160, 161
Bel Geddes, Norman, 71
Bell, James, 139
Bellamy, Ralph, 104
Bender and Daum, 103
Bennett, Bruce, 126, 127, 140, 143
Bennett, Joan, 172, 173
Bennett, Marjorie, 168
Bercovici, Leonardo, 83
Bergman, Ingrid, 19, 20, 120, 121
Berkeley, Busby, 76
Berman, Pandro S., 163
Bernard, Barry, 136
Bernard, Ivor, 161
Bernhardt, Curtis, 131, 156
Best, Willie, 108, 124
Bezzerides, A. J., 107, 156
Biddell, Sidney, 139
*Big City Blues*, 16, 44, 45
*Big Shot, The*, 19, 116, 117
*Big Sleep, The*, 22, 134, 135
Bikel, Theodore, 159
"Billy Dannreuther," 25, 164, 165
Bischoff, Sam, 64, 75, 88, 92, 96
Bishop, Julie, 123
Bissell, Whit, 175

*Black Legion*, 17, 62, 63
Blake, Bobby, 143
Blake, George, 68
Blandick, Clara, 47, 111
Blanke, Henry, 112, 143
Bloch, Bertram, 91
Blondell, Joan, 44, 47, 54, 55, 72
Blue, Monte, 119, 128, 144
*Body And Soul*, 15, 34, 35
Bogart, Belmont, 13
Bogart, Leslie, 11, 22
Bogart, Stephen, 11, 22
Bois, Curt, 80, 120
Bolster, Anita, 136
Bond, David, 156
Bond, Ward, 71, 80, 92, 112
Borg, Veda Ann, 64, 68
Boteler, Wade, 92
Bouchey, Willis B., 160
Bowker, Aldrich, 111
Brackett, Leigh, 135
Bracy, Sidney, 59
Brady, William A., 14
Brady, William A., Jr., 14
Brand, Max, 40
Brando, Marlon, 24
Brandon, Henry, 63
Brazzi, Rossano, 171
Brecher, Egon, 63
Brendel, El, 39
Brennan, Walter, 132, 133
Brent, George, 82, 83, 91
Bressart, Felix, 103
Brewer, George Emerson, Jr., 91
Bricker, George, 87
Bridge, Al, 79
Bridges, Lloyd, 127
Briggs, Donald, 76, 79
Bright, John, 47, 64
*Bright Victory*, 24
Brissac, Virginia, 52, 91, 116
Bromfield, Louis, 103
Brooks, Hadda, 152
Brooks, Richard, 25, 144, 160, 163
Brophy, Edward, 115
*Brother Orchid*, 18, 104, 105
Brown, Charles D., 104, 135
Brown, Harris, 160
Brown, Harry Joe, 60
Brown, James, 151
Brown, Raymond, 87
Brown, Roland, 84
Bruce, Nigel, 136

Brunn, Frederick, 128
Bryan, Jane, 67, 68, 99
Buckner, Robert, 88, 92, 100
"Bugs Fenner," 54, 55
Bull, Peter, 159
*Bullets Or Ballots*, 17, 54, 55
Bupp, Sonny, 75
Bupp, Tommy, 75
Burke, Frankie, 84
Burke, James, 71, 112, 115
Burnett, Murray, 120
Burnett, W. R., 18, 87, 108
Burton, Robert, 176
Bushman, Francis X., 168
Busley, Jessie, 87, 103
Butler, David, 124

Cabot, Susan, 155
Cagney, James, 18, 84, 85, 92, 93, 96, 97
*Caine Mutiny, The*, 25, 166, 167
Caites, Joe, 104
Campana, Nina, 51
Campbell, Colin, 136
Campbell, William, 163
Cane, Charles, 115, 138, 139
Cantor, Eddie, 124
Capote, Truman, 164
"Captain Queeg," 13, 25, 166, 167
Cardwell, James, 148
Carey, Harry, 68
Carmichael, Hoagy, 132
Carnovsky, Morris, 139
Carr, Marion, 179
Carroll, Leo G., 172
Carson, Jack, 72
Carson, James B., 79, 124
Carson, Robert, 119
Carter, Ann, 136
*Casablanca*, 19, 20, 22, 24, 120, 121
Catlett, Walter, 44, 45
Cavanaugh, Hobart, 52, 60
*Chain Lightning*, 23, 150,151
*Chalked Out*, 88
Chan, George, 176
Chan, Spencer, 119
Chandler, Chick, 116, 123
Chandler, Eddie, 96
Chandler, George, 139
Chandler, Raymond, 135
"Charlie Allnut," 13, 24, 158, 159
Charters, Spencer, 79, 108
Chiantoni, Renato, 171
Chin, Sophie, 176

*China Clipper*, 17, 56, 57
Ching, William, 152
Chong, Peter, 176
Christie, Audrey, 160
Christopher, Robert, 171
Christy, Ken, 116
"Chuck Martin," 98, 99
Chung, Doris, 176
Ciannelli, Eduardo, 67, 128
Clark, Cliff, 111
Clark, Dane, 123
Clement, Clay, 52
Clift, Montgomery, 24
Clive, E. E., 59
Cobb, Humphrey, 64
Cobb, Lee J., 156, 176
Colcord, Mabel, 60
Collier, William, Sr., 32
Collins, Ray, 175
Colman, Ronald, 15
Colmans, Edward, 156
Comisky, Pat, 179
Compton, Joyce, 39
*Conflict*, 22, 130, 131
Conlin, Jimmy, 147
Connell, Richard, 104
Conried, Hans, 128
Conway, Morgan, 104
Cook, Elisha, Jr., 112, 135
Cooper, Clancy, 160
Corby, Ellen, 168
Corday, Marcelle, 71
Cording, Harry, 78, 79
Cortesa, Valentina, 171
Cott, Jonathan, 163
*Coup de Grace*, 156
Courtland, Jerome, 148
Courtney, Inez, 44, 45
Cowan, Ashley, 160
Cowan, Jerome, 108, 112
*Cradle Snatchers*, 15
Craig, Alec, 123
Crawford, Broderick, 20
Crehan, Joseph, 55, 56, 68, 88, 95, 96, 104, 160
*Crime School*, 18, 78, 79
Crisp, Donald, 60, 80, 92, 104
Crockett, Luther, 160
Cromwell, John, 139
Cross, Alexander, 56
Cummings, Irving, 31, 40
Cunningham, Joe, 68
Curtis, Alan, 108

Curtiz, Michael, 25, 68, 84, 100, 120, 128, 172
Cutting, Richard, 176

Dale, Carlo, 171
Dale, Esther, 71
Dalio, Marcel, 120, 132, 168
Dalya, Jacqueline, 143
D'Andrea, Tom, 140
Dandridge, Ruby, 139
Dantine, Helmut, 120, 128, 129
*Dark Passage*, 22, 140, 141
*Dark Victory*, 18, 90, 91
Darrin, Sonia, 135
Darwell, Jane, 115
da Silva, Howard, 116
d'Auburn, Dennis, 34, 35
Daves, Delmar, 51, 140
"David Graham," 66, 67
Davidson, William B., 67
Daves, Alan, 67
Davis, Bette, 18, 36, 47, 50, 51, 66, 67, 68, 69, 90, 91, 124
Davis, Johnnie, 76
Davis, Robert A., 147
*Dead End*, 17, 26, 70, 71
*Deadline—U.S.A.*, 25, 160, 161
*Dead Reckoning*, 22, 138, 139
*Death Of A Salesman*, 24
DeCarlo, Vinnie, 179
Decker, Diana, 171
De Corsia, Ted, 155
Deering, John, 96
de Havilland, Olivia, 124
De La Cruz, Joe, 31
Dell, Gabriel, 71, 79, 84
Demarest, William, 115
Dennis, Nick, 156
Derek, John, 146, 147
De Santis, Joseph, 160
*Desperate Hours, The*, 26, 174, 175
*Devil With Women, A*, 15, 30, 31
Devlin, Joe, 92
De Vorska, Jesse, 39
Dickson, Gloria, 82, 83
Dieterle, William, 60
Dillaway, Donald, 35
"Dixon Steele," 13, 23, 152, 153
Dmytryk, Edward, 25, 26, 167, 176
"Dobbs," 13, 23, 24, 142, 143
Dobkin, Larry, 160
Dodd, Claire, 52
Donath, Ludwig, 156

Donde, Manuel, 143
Doniger, Walter, 148
Donnell, Jeff, 152
Donnelly, Ruth, 124
Donovan, King, 155
Dorn, Philip, 128
D'Orsay, Fifi, 39
Doucette, John, 160
Douglas, Don, 123
Downing, Joe, 83, 84, 88, 99, 116
Drake, Charles, 131
Dray, Douglas, 35
Drew, Roland, 116, 119
*Drifting*, 19
Dubov, Paul, 160
Duff, Warren, 84, 92, 99
Dugan, Tom, 44
Duggan, Pat, 172
"Duke Berne," 116, 117
"Duke Mantee," 13, 16, 17, 18, 26, 50,
  51
Dumbrille, Douglass, 100
Dunn, Emma, 36
Dunn, Josephine, 44, 45
Durand, David, 36
Duryea, Dan, 127
*Dust And Sun*, 31
Dvorak, Ann, 46, 47

Eagles, S. P., 159
Eben, Al, 156
"Eddie Willis," 13, 178, 179
Edelman, Louis F., 67, 99
"Ed Hatch," 74, 75
"Ed Hutcheson," 25, 160, 161
Edmunds, William, 116
Eilers, Sally, 40, 41
Eisner, June, 160
Elderbloom Chorus, The, 103
Eldredge, John, 87, 108
Elliott, Robert, 96
Ellis, Patricia, 47
Elsom, Isobel, 136
Emery, Gilbert, 55
*Enforcer, The*, 23, 154, 155
Enright, Ray, 56, 75, 111
Epstein, Julius J., 120
Epstein, Philip G., 120
Erskine, Chester, 48
Evans, Bob, 68
Evans, Vincent, 151
Eyer, Richard, 175

Fadden, Tom, 135
Farrell, Charlie, 15, 35
Farrell, Glenda, 47
Faulkner, William, 132, 135
Faye, Herbie, 179
Faylen, Frank, 55, 68
Fazenda, Louise, 74, 75
Fellows, Robert, 100
Fernandez, Abel, 179
Ferrer, José, 167
Fessier, Michael, 103
Fields, Stanley, 40
Finkel, Abem, 63, 67, 116
Finn, Jonathan, 88, 99
Fisher, Steve, 139
Fitzgerald, Geraldine, 91
Flavin, James, 131, 135
Flick, Pat C., 63
Flint, Helen, 48, 63
*Flirt, The*, 36
Flynn, Errol, 100, 124
Flynn, Gertrude, 171
Fong, Benson, 176
Foo, Lee Tung, 119
Foran, Dick, 51, 63
Forbes, Don, 176
Ford, John, 32
Ford, Wally, 115, 139
Forester, C. S., 159
Forrest, William, 139, 160
Foster, Art, 123
Fox, Sidney, 36, 37, 48, 49
Foy, Charley, 87, 111
Francen, Victor, 128
Francine, Bette, 160
Francis, Kay, 86, 87
Francis, Noel, 32
Francis, Robert, 167
"Frank M'Cloud," 144, 145
Frank, Melvin, 124
"Frank Taylor," 62, 63
"Frank Wilson," 88, 89
Franz, Arthur, 167
Fraser, Bill, 171
Freed, Bert, 175
Freeland, Thornton, 43
Freeman, Everett, 124
French, Valerie, 12
Fuchs, Daniel, 116
Furthman, Jules, 132, 135

Gabel, Martin, 160

Gamet, Kenneth, 88
Gan, Chester, 119
"Garboni," 48, 49
Gardner, Ava, 170, 171
Garfield, John, 124
Gargan, Ed, 79
Garland, Judy, 12
Garnett, Tay, 72
Garrett, Oliver H. P., 139
"Geoffrey Carroll," 136, 137
George, Gladys, 96, 112
"George Hally," 96, 97
Gerald, Jim, 171
Geray, Steven, 152
Gerry, Alex, 160
Gilbert, Edwin, 115
Gillette, Betty, 44
Gillette, Ruth, 152
Gilpatrick, Guy, 123
Glasmon, Kubec, 47
Glass, Everett, 160
Gleason, Jackie C., 115
Gleason, Pat, 104
"Glenn Griffin," 26, 174, 175
"Gloves Donahue," 114, 115
Godfrey, Peter, 136
Gombell, Minna, 108
Gomez, Thomas, 144
Gondo, Gene, 148
Goodis, David, 140
Goodwin, Harold, 148
Gorcey, Leo, 71, 79, 84, 99
Gordon, Bobby, 52
Gordon, C. Henry, 72
Gordon, Mary, 60
Gordon, Ruth, 123
Goring, Marius, 171
Got, Roland, 119
Goulding, Edmund, 91
Graetz, Paul, 58, 59
Grahame, Gloria, 152, 153
Grapewin, Charley, 51
"Grasselli," 102, 103
*Great O'Malley, The*, 17, 60, 61
Greenleaf, Raymond, 160
Greenstreet, Sydney, 112, 113, 118, 119,
  120, 128, 129, 130, 131
Gruning, Ilka, 120
Guilfoyle, Paul, 104

Haade, William, 68, 69, 99
Haines, William Wister, 63
Hale, Alan, 100, 107, 123, 124

Hale, Creighton, 95, 123, 136
Hall, Huntz, 71, 79, 84, 95
Hall, James Norman, 128
Hall, Porter, 51
Hall, Thurston, 80
Halop, Billy, 71, 79, 84, 88, 89
Halton, Charles, 63, 119
Hamilton, Hale, 14, 43, 47
Hamilton, John, 96, 112, 116, 119
Hammett, Dashiell, 112
Hampden, Walter, 168
Han, Otto, 148
Hankinson, Hank, 68
Hanlon, Bert, 80
"Hap Stuart," 56, 57
Harbord, Carl, 127
*Harder They Fall, The*, 11, 27, 178, 179
Harlan, Kenneth, 56, 57
Harmer, Lillian, 60
Harrigan, Nedda, 76
Harris, Sybil, 79
"Harry Dawes," 13, 26, 170, 171
"Harry Galleon," 76, 77
"Harry Morgan," 21, 132, 133
"Harry Smith," 156, 157
Hart, Gordon, 59, 60
Harvey, Lew, 92
Harvey, Paul, 51, 63, 108
Hatton, Raymond, 67
Hawks, Howard, 21, 132, 133, 135
Hayakawa, Sessue, 148
Hayden, Harry, 52, 63
Hayes, Alfred, 176
Hayes, Joseph, 175
Hayes, Sam, 108
Heggie, O. P., 48
Heisler, Stuart, 148, 151
Hellinger, Mark, 96, 103, 104, 107, 108, 124, 136
Hellman, Lillian, 17, 71
*Hell's Bells*, 15
Helm, Fay, 83, 91
Helvick, James, 164
Hemingway, Ernest, 132
Henley, Hobart, 36
Henreid, Paul, 120
Henry, Thomas Browne, 160
Hepburn, Audrey, 26, 168, 169
Hepburn, Katharine, 24, 158, 159
Herbert, Hugh, 76
Herman, Tommy, 179
Hern, Pepe, 147
Heyburn, Weldon, 79

Heydt, Louis Jean, 135
Hickman, Howard, 52, 95, 103
Hicks, Russell, 160
*High Sierra*, 18, 108, 109
Hill, Al, 64
Hillaire, Marcel, 168
Hinds, Samuel, 63
Hobart, Rose, 131
Hobbes, Halliwell, 43
Hogan, Dick, 123
Holden, William, 18, 98, 99, 168
Holt, Tim, 143
*Holy Terror, A*, 15, 40, 41
Homans, Robert, 80
Hoo, Walter Soo, 176
Hopkins, Arthur, 16
Hopkins, Miriam, 100
Hopper, DeWolf, 95
Horman, Arthur T., 131
Horne, John, 171
Horton, Edward Everett, 124
Howard, Frances, 14
Howard, Joan, 75
Howard, Leslie, 16, 50, 51, 72, 73
Howard, Lewis, 152
Howland, Jobyna, 44
Howlin, Olin, 75, 95
Huber, Harold, 88
Hughes, Dorothy B., 152
Hull, Henry, 48, 49, 108
Humbert, George, 71
Hume, Cyril, 148
Humphrey, Maud, 13
Hunter, Kim, 160
Husson, Albert, 172
Huston, John, 12, 13, 18, 19, 22, 23, 24, 25, 27, 80, 108, 112, 119, 143, 144, 159, 164
Huston, Walter, 142, 143
Hyer, Martha, 168
Hymer, Warren, 32

*In A Lonely Place*, 23, 152, 153
Inescort, Frieda, 60
Ingram, Rex, 127
Interlenghi, Franco, 171
*Invisible Stripes*, 18, 98, 99
*Invitation To A Murder*, 16
*Isle Of Fury*, 17, 58, 59
*It All Came True*, 18, 102, 103
*It's A Wise Child*, 15

"Jack Buck," 104, 105

Jackson, Horace, 76
Jackson, Selmer, 160
Jackson, Thomas, 44, 135
Jacobs, William, 59, 131
Jacoby, Hans, 156
Jacoby, Michel, 52
"James Frazier," 84, 85
Jaquet, Frank, 79
Jason, Sybil, 60
Jenkins, Allen, 46, 47, 67, 70, 71, 75, 80, 81, 83, 104
Jewell, Isabel, 67, 108
"Jim Carmody," 26, 27, 176, 177
Jiminez, Soledad, 68
"Jim Leonard," 42, 43
"Jim Watson," 34, 35
Job, Thomas, 136
"Joe Barrett," 148, 149
"Joe Gurney," 86, 87
"Joe 'Red' Kennedy," 64, 65
"Joe Rossi," 122, 123
"John Murrell," 100, 101
"John Phillips," 60, 61
Johnson, Henry M., 31
Johnson, Moffat, 48
Johnson, Van, 167
Joiner, Pat, 155
Jones, Dickie, 63, 100
Jones, Gordon, 148
Jones, Jennifer, 164
Jones, Spike, 124
Jordan, Bobby, 71, 79, 84
"Joseph," 26, 172, 173
Judels, Charles, 39, 103

Kama, Kyoko, 148
Karns, Roscoe, 107
Katz, Lee, 95
Keane, Edward, 96, 160
Keighley, William, 55
Keith, Robert, 163
Kelland, Clarence, 72
Kellaway, Cecil, 104
Kelley, Barry, 147
Kellogg, John, 155
Kelly, Paul, 96, 99
Kendall, Cy, 78, 79
Kennedy, Arthur, 24, 108, 109, 175
Kennedy, Douglas, 140
Kennedy, Jack, 43
Kent, Crauford, 35
Kenyon, Charles, 51
Kern, James V., 124

Kerr, Laura, 163
Kerrigan, J. M., 123
Kessel, Joseph, 156
*Key Largo*, 23, 144, 145
Kibbee, Guy, 44
*Kid Galahad*, 17, 68, 69
Kilian, Victor, 100
Kimble, Lawrence, 103
King, Joseph, 55, 56, 64, 88, 116
*King Of The Underworld*, 18, 86, 87
King, Owen, 56
Kingsford, Guy, 127
Kingsley, Sidney, 17, 71
Kinney, Harold, 35
Kinskey, Leonid, 120
Kirkwood, James, 40
Klein, Adelaide, 155
Klein, Wally, 92
Knapp, Evalyn, 44
*Knock On Any Door*, 23, 146, 147
Knowlden, Marilyn, 84
Knox, Alexander, 148, 149
Knox, Mickey, 147
Knudsen, Peggy, 135
Kolker, Henry, 55
Komai, Tetsu, 59, 148
Korda, Zoltan, 127
Kosleck, Martin, 115
Kramer, Stanley, 167
Kranz, Jack, 68
Kreuger, Kurt, 127
Krims, Milton, 60
Kulp, Nancy, 168
Kumagai, Frank, 148

Lackteen, Frank, 59
Lady Killers' Quartet, The, 103
Lambert, Jack, 155
Landi, Elissa, 35
Lane, Lola, 67
Lane, Mike, 179
Lane, Priscilla, 76, 77, 96
Lane, Richard, 104
Lane, Rosemary, 92, 95
Lane, Rusty, 179
Langan, Glenn, 95
La Roy, Rita, 40
La Torre, Charles, 128
Lawes, Joan, 32
Lawes, Lewis E., 88, 99
Lawrence, Marc, 64, 99, 144
Lawson, John Howard, 123, 127
LeBeau, Madeleine, 120

Lee, Bernard, 164
Lee, George, 176
*Left Hand Of God, The*, 26, 176, 177
Lehman, Ernest, 168
Lentok, Leon, 176
Leo, Maurice, 75
Leonard, Barbara, 43
Leonard, Sheldon, 132
Le Roy, Mervyn, 44, 47
Leslie, Joan, 108, 111, 124
Levene, Sam, 123
Lewis, David, 91
Lewis, Harry, 144
Lewis, Vera, 95, 96
Linden, Eric, 44
Lindsay, Margaret, 58, 59
"Linus Larabee," 26, 168, 169
Litel, John, 63, 67, 80, 88, 95, 100, 103, 107
Litvak, Anatole, 80
Lloyd, George, 64
Lockhart, Gene, 76
Lockhart, Kathleen, 76
Loder, John, 128
Lollobrigida, Gina, 164
Longmire, Adele, 163
Loo, Richard, 119
Lord, Robert, 63, 80, 147, 148, 152, 156
Lorre, Peter, 20, 112, 113, 115, 120, 128, 129, 164, 165
*Love Affair*, 16, 42, 43
Love, Bessie, 171
Lovejoy, Frank, 152
Lowe, Edmund, 38, 39
Loy, Myrna, 35
Lucas, Wilfred, 104
Luce, Claire, 32, 33
Luft, Sid, 12
Lugosi, Bela, 39
Luke, Keye, 119
Luna, Margarito, 143
Lupino, Ida, 18, 107, 108, 109, 124
Lyndon, Barre, 80
Lynn, Jeffrey, 96, 103
Lynn, Sharon, 32
Lynn, Stella, 176
Lys, Lya, 94, 95

Macaulay, Richard, 96, 107, 119
MacBride, Donald, 108
MacDonald, Philip, 127
MacDougall, Ranald, 172
MacFarlane, George, 32

Mackaill, Dorothy, 42, 43
MacKellar, Helen, 52, 79
MacKenzie, Joyce, 160
MacLane, Barton, 54, 55, 64, 108, 112, 115, 143
MacLaren, Ian, 35
MacMurray, Fred, 167
Macready, George, 147
Main, Marjorie, 71
"Major Jed Webbe," 25, 162, 163
Makin, William J., 95
Mallinson, Rory, 140
Malone, Dorothy, 135
*Maltese Falcon, The*, 18, 19, 24, 112, 113
Mankiewicz, Joseph L., 25, 26, 171
Manning, Irene, 116, 117
*Man Who Came Back, The*, 15
March, Fredric, 24, 174, 175
Marion, Paul, 132
Maris, Mona, 30, 31
"Mark Braden," 78, 79
*Marked Woman*, 17, 19, 66, 67
Marly, Florence, 148, 149
Marquis, Rosalind, 66, 67
"Marshall Canc," 94, 95
Marshall, E. G., 167, 176, 177
Marshall, Tully, 72, 99
Marston, John, 47
"Martin," 17, 82, 83
Martin, Dewey, 147, 174, 175
"Martin Ferguson," 154, 155
Marvin, Lee, 167
Massey, Raymond, 122, 123, 151
"Matrac," 128, 129
"Matt Brennan," 150, 151
Matthews, Allen, 67
Matthews, Lester, 119
Maugham, Somerset, 59
Mayer, Louis B., 22
Mayo, Archie L., 16, 51, 63
Mayo, Frank, 111
McCrea, Ann, 160
McCrea, Joel, 70, 71
McDaniel, Hattie, 124
McDaniel, Sam, 115
McDonald, Frank, 59
McGann, William, 52
McHugh, Frank, 55, 74, 75, 96, 100, 114, 115
McKenna, Ken, 15
McLaglen, Victor, 15, 31, 38, 39
McWade, Edward, 44
Mell, Joe, 160

Meeker, George, 96, 108
*Meet The Wife*, 15
Melton, Sid, 147
*Men Are Such Fools*, 18, 76, 77
Mencken, Helen, 19
Mercier, Louis, 127, 128
Meredith, Charles, 148
Methot, Mayo, 19, 20, 21, 66, 67
"Michael O'Leary," 90, 91
Michel, Lora Lee, 148
Middlemas, Robert, 52
Middleton, Charles, 92, 100
Middleton, Robert, 175
*Midnight*, 16, 48, 49
Miljan, Trevor, 92
Miller, Marvin, 139
Miller, Seton I., 55, 68
Millhauser, Bertram, 116, 148
Milne, Peter, 64
Ming, Moy, 176
Minjir, Harold, 43
Mitchell, Grant, 44, 47, 103, 131
Moffitt, Jack, 128
Mohr, Gerald, 156
Molnar, Walter, 132
Monohan, Richard, 160
Mong, William V., 72
Monks, John, Jr., 147
Montalban, Carlos, 179
Montgomery, Goodee, 32
Montgomery, Ray, 123
Mooney, Martin, 55
Moore, Carlyle, Jr., 52, 56
Moore, Dennis, 56
Moore, Sue, 75
Moorhead, Agnes, 140, 176
Moraine, Lyle, 56
Moran, Dolores, 132
Morehouse, Ward, 44
Morgan, Dennis, 94, 95, 124
Morgan, Michele, 128
Mori, Hideo, 148
Morita, Miki, 59
Morley, Robert, 159, 164, 165
Morris, Adrian, 51, 84
Morris, Wayne, 56, 68, 69, 76, 94, 95
Morrison, Ann, 163
Mostel, Zero, 154, 155, 156
Motley, Willard, 147
Mowbray, Alan, 72
Mower, Jack, 79, 95, 111
Mudie, Leonard, 91
Mura, Corinna, 120, 128

Murphy, Mary, 175
Murphy, Matt, 179

Nadi, Aldo, 132
Nagel, Anne, 56
Nagel, Conrad, 36, 37
Naish, J. Carrol, 127
Negley, Howard, 160
*Nerves*, 15
Nestell, Bob, 68
Neuman, Alfred, 131
Niblo, Fred, Jr., 111
Nichols, Dudley, 31
Nicholson, Kenyon, 75
"Nick Coster," 18, 110, 111
Nissen, Greta, 39
Nolan, James, 76
Nordhoff, Charles, 128
North, Edmund H., 152
Nugent, J. C., 72
Nugent, Richard, 127

O'Brien, Edmond, 170, 171
O'Brien, George, 40, 41
O'Brien, Liam, 151
O'Brien, Pat, 56, 57, 60, 61, 64, 65, 84
O'Brien-Moore, Erin, 62, 63
O'Connell, Hugh, 75
O'Connor, Una, 103
Offerman, George, Jr., 79, 123
O'Flynn, Damian, 67
O'Hanlon, James, 127
*Oklahoma Kid, The*, 18, 92, 93
Oliver, Gordon, 64
Olsen, Moroni, 99, 100
O'Moore, Patrick, 127, 131, 136
O'Neill, Henry, 48, 52, 60, 67, 80, 83, 99, 107
Orlandi, Felice, 179
Orth, Frank, 52
Ortiz, Peter, 156
Orzazewski, Kasia, 160
O'Shea, Oscar, 83
Otto, Frank, 79
Overman, Lynne, 48, 49
Owen, Garry, 64, 111
Owen, Tudor, 160

Paduan, Anna Maria, 171
Page, Bradley, 43
Page, Gale, 79, 80, 88, 106, 107
Page, Joy, 120
Panama, Norman, 124

Paramore, Edward E., 92
Paris, Jerry, 167
Parker, Eleanor, 150, 151
Parnell, Emory, 168
Parrish, John, 171
Parrott, Ursulla, 43
*Passage To Marseille*, 22, 128, 129
Patrick, Lee, 99, 112
"Paul Fabrini," 106, 107
Pawley, Edward, 84, 92
Pawley, William, 55, 64
Peck, Charles, 71
Pendleton, Gaylord, 32
Pendleton, Nat, 74, 75
Penman, Lea, 172
Perry, Linda, 52
Perry, Susan, 146, 147
Persoff, Nehemiah, 178, 179
Peters, Susan, 116
Peterson, Dorothy, 91
*Petrified Forest, The*, 16, 17, 50, 51
Phelps, Buster, 46, 47
"Philip Marlowe," 134, 135
Phillips, Mary, 19
Phillips, Paul, 104
Pingree, Earl, 40
Pitts, Zasu, 36, 103
*Place In The Sun, A*, 24
Porcasi, Paul, 79
Porter, Jean, 176
Powers, Tom, 160
Price, Alonzo, 63
Prince, William, 139
Prior, J. Redmond, 151
Puglia, Frank, 120, 123
Punsley, Bernard, 71, 79, 84
Purcell, Richard, 55

Qualen, John, 120
Quan, Henry S., 176
"Quintain," 72, 73

Rabagliati, Alberto, 171
*Racket Busters*, 18, 82, 83
Rackin, Martin, 155
Rafferty, Tom, 135
Raft, George, 18, 99, 106, 107
Raine, Norman Reilly, 76
Rains, Claude, 120, 121, 128
Ralston, Marcia, 76
Rangel, A. Soto, 143
Rathbone, Basil, 172
Rawlinson, Herbert, 55, 88, 91

Ray, Aldo, 172, 173
Ray, Nicholas, 147, 152
Reagan, Ronald, 75, 91
Red Wing, Rodric, 144
Reed, Alan, 175
Reed, Tom, 60
Regas, George, 59
Reicher, Frank, 60
Reid, Carl Benton, 152, 176
Reilly, Tommy, 103
Remley, Ralph, 55, 87
Renna, Vincent, 156
*Return Of Dr. X, The*, 18, 94, 95
Reynolds, Craig, 60
Reynolds, Jack, 152
Reynolds, Joyce, 124
Riano, Reine, 76
"Richard Mason," 130, 131
Richards, Addison, 56, 63
Richards, Stephen, 128
Richman, Charles, 91
Richmond, Kane, 123
"Rick," 13, 24, 120, 121
"Rick Leland," 118, 119
Rico, Mona, 31
Riddell, Sidney, 139
Ridgely, John, 88, 95, 104, 111, 116, 135
Ridges, Stanley, 116
Rioli, Riccardo, 171
Ripley, Clement, 31
"Rip Murdock," 138, 139
Risdon, Elizabeth, 71, 96, 108
Rivkin, Allen, 139, 163
Roach, Bert, 36
*Roaring Twenties, The*, 18, 96, 97
Robbins, James, 64, 67
Roberts, Allene, 147
Roberts, Beverly, 52, 53, 56
Roberts, Roy, 151, 155
Roberts, Stanley, 167
Robinson, Casey, 91, 128
Robinson, Charles, 75
Robinson, Edward G., 16, 17, 18, 54, 55, 68, 69, 80, 81, 104, 105, 144, 145
Robinson, Ruth, 56
Robles, Rudy, 119
Robson, Flora, 99
Robson, Mark, 25, 179
"Rocks Valentine," 80, 81
Rodney, John, 144
Roope, Fay, 160
Rosenbloom, Maxie, 80, 81
Ross, Leonard Q., 115

Rossen, Robert, 67, 83, 96
"Rossi, Joe," 122, 123
Rowan, Don, 83, 104
Roy, Billy, 128
"Roy Earle," 13, 18, 108, 109
Rumann, Sig, 111
Ryan, Don, 88
Ryan, Tim, 104

*Sabrina*, 26, 168, 169
*Sabrina Fair*, 168
*Sahara*, 22, 126, 127
Sakall, S. Z., 120, 124, 125
Sale, Virginia, 116
"Sam Spade," 13, 19, 112, 113
Sande, Walter, 132, 133
San Martin, Raymond, 67
*San Quentin*, 17, 64, 65
Santell, Alfred, 35
Saper, Jack, 119
*Saturday's Children*, 15
Savage, Daniel Boone, 75
Sawyer, Joseph, 51, 63, 64, 88, 96, 160
Sayles, Francis, 63
Schrank, Joseph, 75
Schulberg, Budd, 179
Schumann-Heink, Ferdinand, 52
Schumm, Hans, 115, 127
Schwartz, Arthur, 124
Scott, Lizabeth, 139
Scott, Martha, 174, 175
Scott, Randolph, 100, 101
Scott, Wallace, 116
Seidner, Irene, 115
Seiler, Lewis, 79, 87, 88, 103, 116
Sellars, Elizabeth, 171
Selwart, Tonio, 171
Servoss, Mary, 131
Seymour, Dan, 120, 132, 133, 144
"Sgt. Joe Gunn," 126, 127
Shay, Patricia, 132
Shayne, Konstantine, 128
Shea, Gloria, 44
Sheehan, John,
Sheehan, Perry, 67, 163
Shelton, Marla, 72
Sheridan, Ann, 18, 60, 63, 64, 65, 84, 102, 103, 106, 107, 124
Sheridan, Frank, 60
Sherman, Fred, 151
Sherman, Vincent, 79, 87, 95, 115
"Sherry Scott," 52, 53
Sherwood, Robert E., 16, 51

Shimada, Teru, 148
Shirley, Florence, 160
Shore, Dinah, 124
Sidney, Sylvia, 71, 110, 111
Siegel, Sol C., 160
Sifton, Claire, 48
Sifton, Paul, 48
Siletti, Mario, 155
Silverheels, Jay, 144
Silvers, Phil, 115
Simpson, Russell, 100
Sinatra, Frank, 12
Singleton, Penny, 75, 76, 83
Siodmak, Robert, 131
Sir Lancelot, 132
*Sirocco*, 23, 156, 157
*Skyrocket*, 15
Sloane, Everett, 155, 156
Smith, Alexis, 124, 131, 136
Smith, Art, 152
Smith, Emmett, 132
Smith, John, 172
Sokoloff, Vladimir, 80, 128
Solt, Andrew, 152
Somerset, Pat, 35
Sothern, Ann, 104
Sothern, Hugh, 92
Soubier, Clifford, 63
Sparks, Ned, 44, 45
Sperling, Milton, 155
Spigelgass, Leonard, 115
*Squadrons*, 35
Staiola, Enzo, 171
*Stand-In*, 17, 72, 73
Stanley, Edwin, 67, 131
Stanton, Paul, 63, 119
Stanwyck, Barbara, 136, 137
St. Brendan's Church Choir, 84
Steele, Bob, 135
Steiger, Rod, 178, 179
Stephens, Harvey, 88, 92
Stephenson, James, 86, 87
Sterling, Jan, 179
"Steve," 32, 33
"Steve Nash," 40, 41
Stevens, Onslow, 156
Stevens, Warren, 160, 171
Stevenson, Houseley, 59
Stevenson, Houseley, Jr., 140
Stevenson, Tom, 119
Stevenson, Margot, 99
Stewart, Martha, 152
Stewart, Paul, 160

"Stone," 38, 39
Stone, George E., 55, 88
Stone, Harold J., 179
Stone, Milburn, 56
Stone, Paula, 52
Stossel, Ludwig, 115, 120, 123
St. Polis, John, 31, 155
Strange, Robert, 67, 108
*Streetcar Named Desire, A*, 24
Sullivan, Elliot, 83, 123
Sully, Frank, 115
Summerville, Slim, 36
Swanick, Peter, 159
Swerling, Jo, 43
*Swifty*, 14
*Swing Your Lady*, 18, 74, 75

Talbot, Gloria, 172
Talbot, Lyle, 44, 45, 47
Talton, Alice, 152
Taradash, Daniel, 147
Tarkington, Booth, 36
Tasker, Robert, 64
Taylor, Dwight, 131
Taylor, Samuel, 168
Teal, Ray, 175
Terry, Phil, 160
Terry, Sheila, 44, 45, 47
*Thank Your Lucky Stars*, 22, 124, 125
*They Drive By Night*, 18, 106, 107
*Thirteen, The*, 127
Thomas, Frankie, 99
Thompson, Harlan, 111
Thompson, Slim, 51
*Three On A Match*, 16, 46, 47
Tiernan, Patricia, 163
Tierney, Gene, 176
Tobias, George, 107, 124, 128, 129
Tobin, Genevieve, 51
*To Have And Have Not*, 21, 22, 132, 133
*Tokyo Joe*, 23, 148, 149
Tolan, Michael, 155
"Tom Standish," 30, 31
Tong, Kam, 119
Toomey, Regis, 135
Toren, Marta, 156, 157
Torvay, José, 143
Towne, Gene, 72
Toy, Noel, 176
Tracy, Spencer, 15, 32, 33
Tracy, William, 84
*Trailin'*, 40

Traven, B., 143
Travers, Henry, 88, 91, 108
Travis, Richard, 116
*Treasure Of The Sierra Madre, The*, 22, 23, 24, 142, 143
Trevor, Claire, 71, 80, 81, 144, 145
Trivers, Barry, 111
Trobridge, Charles, 79
Tsien, Marie, 176
Tsuruta, Yosan, 148
Tucker, Harland, 68, 87
Tucker, Richard, 40
Tulli, Marco, 164, 165
Tully, Tom, 167
"Turkey Morgan," 13, 68, 69
*Two Against The World*, 17, 52, 53
*Two Mrs. Carrolls, The*, 22, 136, 137
Tyler, Harry, 160
Tyler, Tom, 104
Tynan, Brendon, 103

Underdown, Edward, 164
*Up The River*, 15, 32, 33
Usher, Guy, 67
Ustinov, Peter, 172, 173

Vale, Martin, 136
"Valentine Corliss," 36, 37
Vallon, Nanette, 104
"Val Stevens," 58, 59
Vaughan, Dorothy, 63
Vavitch, Michael, 31
Veidt, Conrad, 115, 120
Veiller, Anthony, 151
Verne, Kaaren, 115
Vernon, Irene, 160
Vickers, Martha, 135
Vigran, Herbert, 103
"Vincent Parry," 140, 141
*Virginia City*, 18, 100, 101
Vogan, Emmett, 64
Vohs, Joan, 168
Von Eltz, Theodore, 135
Vuolo, Tito, 155

Wagner, Max, 64, 96
*Wagons Roll At Night, The*, 18, 110, 111
Walcott, Jersey Joe, 179
Wald, Jerry, 96, 107, 115, 119, 123, 140, 144
Waldron, Charles, 135
Walker, Nella, 168

Wallace, Dan, 135
Wallace, Francis, 68, 111
Wallis, Hal B., 60, 64, 67, 75, 80, 88, 91, 92, 96, 99, 100, 103, 104, 107, 108, 112, 115, 120, 128
Wallis, Norman, 83
Walsh, Raoul, 18, 39, 96, 107, 108
Walthall, Henry B., 56
Wanger, Walter, 17, 72
Warner, Jack, 17, 22
Warren, Bruce, 35
Warren, Katharine, 167
Warren, Ruth, 152
Warwick, Robert, 40, 152
Watkins, Maurine, 32
Watson, Delmar, 60
Watson, Minor, 71, 116, 123
Wayne, Billy, 80
Wead, Frank, 56
Weaver, Elviry, 75
Weaver, Frank, 75
Weaver, Leon, 75
Weaver, Marjorie, 56
Weitsenkorn, Louis, 52
Welden, Ben, 67, 68, 115, 135
Wengraf, John, 127
*We're No Angels*, 26, 172, 173
Wessell, Dick, 104, 123
West, Pat, 132
Wexley, John, 80, 84
"Whip McCord," 92, 93
White, Marjorie, 39
White, Sammy, 75
*White Sister, The*, 15
White and Stanley, 103
Whitney, Peter, 123
Whorf, Richard, 48, 151
Wilbur, Crane, 79
Wilcox, Frank, 100, 111, 119, 131
Wilde, Cornel, 108
Wilder, Billy, 25, 26, 168
Wilkins, Martin, 156
William, Warren, 47
Williams, Cara, 147
Williams, Guinn, 100
Williams, John, 168
Williams, Lottie, 91
Williams, Rhys, 148
Williams, Sumner, 147
Willis, Norman, 55
Wilson, Charles, 55, 95
Wilson, Don, 124
Wilson, Dooley, 120

Wilson, Katherine, 48
Wilson, Marie, 56
Windust, Bretaigne, 155
Winninger, Charles, 36
Witherspoon, Cora, 48, 91
*Women Of All Nations*, 15, 38, 39
Wong, Beal, 176
Wong, Stephen, 176
Wood, Douglas, 52
Woods, Donald, 59

Wouk, Herman, 167
Wren, Sam, 67
Wright, William, 56
Wycherly, Margaret, 48
Wyler, William, 17, 25, 26, 71, 174, 175
Wynn, Keenan, 163
Wynn, May, 167

Yong, Soo, 176
Yordan, Philip, 179

*You Can't Get Away With Murder*, 18, 88, 89
Young, Carlton, 160
Young, Clifton, 140
Young, Gig, 175
Yung, Victor Sen, 119, 176

Zanoli, Maria, 171
Zanuck, Darryl, 22